PENGUIN BOOKS
SRI SIDDHI MA

Dr Jaya Prasada was born on 13 August 1948 in Lucknow. She graduated from Loreto College, and earned her master's degree from the University of Lucknow. In 1981, she did her PhD on Prime Minister Indira Gandhi from the University of Rohilkhand.

Prasada lived for thirty-seven years in the closest proximity to the divine mother Sri Siddhi Ma, who inherited the spiritual legacy of Neem Karoli Baba. Her debut book is dedicated to her guru Sri Siddhi Ma and takes us into the life and times of the silent saint of Kainchi.

Prasada lives between Kainchi Dham and her home 'Teertham' in Nainital, where Sri Siddhi Ma took mahasamadhi in December 2017.

She is an ardent photographer, a keen mountain traveller and likes to keep up with technology.

PRAISE FOR THE BOOK

'This book is like a benediction—an extraordinary account of the journey of faith and devotion that led Jaya Prasada to Sri Siddhi Ma, the silent saint of Kainchi'—Namita Gokhale, author, co-founder, Jaipur Literature Festival

'The relationship between Guru and Shishya—teacher and student—is mysterious, intimate and imbued with love. Jaya's book is a "not to be missed gift", sharing her unique experience in this beautifully written tribute to Siddhi Ma, who combined the transcendent legacy of Neem Karoli Baba with the purity of her devotion'—Dr Larry Brilliant, world-renowned physician and epidemiologist

'Shri Siddhi Ma was a great saint of our time. And like Hanuman to Lord Rama, Jaya Prasada dedicated her entire life to serving Ma. Having seen Siddhi Ma for decades from close quarters, there is no better person than Jaya to tell the remarkable story of Ma's divine life, traversed under the grace of her guru, Maharaj ji'—Dr G. Natchiar, Director-Emeritus, Aravind Eye Care System

'Only Jaya's profound love and heart connection with Ma would have allowed her to share these memories with so much depth and sweetness . . . to read them is to receive Mother's grace'—Marlene Roeder, former president, Ram Dass Tape Library Foundation

The Story of
NEEM KAROLI BABA'S
Spiritual Legacy

PENGUIN BOOKS
An imprint of Penguin Random House

PENGUIN BOOKS

USA | Canada | UK | Ireland | Australia
New Zealand | India | South Africa | China

Penguin Books is part of the Penguin Random House group of companies
whose addresses can be found at global.penguinrandomhouse.com

Published by Penguin Random House India Pvt. Ltd
4th Floor, Capital Tower 1, MG Road,
Gurugram 122 002, Haryana, India

First published in Penguin Books by Penguin Random House India 2022

10 9 8 7 6 5 4 3 2 1

The views and opinions expressed in this book are the author's own and the
facts are as reported by her which have been verified to the extent possible,
and the publishers are not in any way liable for the same.

ISBN 9780143457831

Typeset in Adobe Garamond Pro by Manipal Technologies Limited, Manipal

www.penguin.co.in

This book is dedicated to my mother,
Premila Jyoti Prasada, the guiding light of my life

Radhe tu bad bhagini
Kaun tapasya keen
Teen lok taaran tarana
Soh tere aadheen

[Radhe, how blessed you are
What tapasya did you do?
That the redeemer of the three worlds
Is subservient to you.]

—Neem Karoli Baba to Sri Siddhi Ma

A Note to the Reader

I am no writer or historian. For the last forty years, I have spent my life in devotion and service to my guru, Sri Siddhi Ma, the greatest disciple of Maharaj Neem Karoli Baba, and the upholder of his spiritual legacy after he took mahasamadhi in 1973. On this spiritual path, her constant companion was Sri Jivanti Mataji, or Chhoti Ma as she was called, who had been chosen by Maharaj ji himself to be Ma's strength and shield in the world. This book is the story of my life with Ma and Jivanti Mataji. Its pages are also deeply infused with the essence of Maharaj ji. After all, Ma had completely merged her being with Maharaj ji's, and even though my darshans of him were limited to my childhood and youth, I do believe that it was he who shepherded me to Ma.

The concept of 'tyaag' or renunciation is considered synonymous with sacrifices and hardships. But for me, from the moment I saw Ma for the first time in July 1980, at the ashram in Kainchi, it was instant liberation—joyous liberation—from the mores and conventions of the world. The next few decades were spent immersed in the bliss of that divine proximity. Like a toddler with unsteady steps, I held Ma's hands on a journey that revealed so many wonders that left, in their wake, so many insights.

The lives of saints are invariably layered by many veils. They cannot be expressed or revealed using the frames of reference we mortals are used to. A true renunciate cuts off all ties with the world and burns the preceding life in the fire of wisdom. As a devotee, writing a book about my spiritual preceptors, I therefore found myself constrained by a few of these norms. It was not my place to probe their past. What little I have shared of Maharaj ji's earlier life was gleaned from Ma's own telling, and of Ma's earlier life, from anecdotes recounted by Jivanti Mataji and other devotees who had been Ma's contemporaries.

After that first meeting with Ma, I found that my heart was in Kainchi all the time. My physical transition to the ashram, however, took place slowly, days becoming weeks becoming months, until the ashram in Kainchi felt like my home, and I found that I had become an inseparable attendant of Ma and Jivanti Mataji. There was a quiet beauty to the daily rhythm of life with the mothers in the ashram, the seasons giving way gently to the familiar celebrations each year: kirtan in April, the bhandaara in June, guru purnima celebrations with beautiful recitations of the *Ramcharitmanas* in July, the ten-day Devi-paath during Navratri. Several times a year, the mothers also travelled to shrines, near and far, and these journeys to different parts of India gave me glimpses of Ma's profound simplicity and her divine leelas.

And in this way, thirty-seven years flew past.

Ma took mahasamadhi in December 2017. After decades, I suddenly found myself with time on my hands. This led me to reflect on the extraordinary life I had lived with the mothers and this is when the book began to take shape in my mind. Strange as it might seem, many devotees of Maharaj ji had not met Ma in his lifetime, and became aware of her presence only after his mahasamadhi when Ma stepped out of the inner world of the ashram. Even those who came into her fold were unaware of many aspects of her life. It was almost in answer to all their questions that I began to write these pages that are now in your hands.

And as everything else in my life has been, this little book too is an offering of love to Ma, my sadguru.

Jaya Prasada
Teertham, Nainital
March 2022

Part I

Chapter 1

Like so many miracles, like so many mysteries, Neem Karoli Baba and Sri Siddhi Ma entered my life long before I became aware of their divine presence.

I remember, it was the late 1970s and I was working on my PhD thesis that looked at the socio-economic implications of a decade of Indira Gandhi's term as Prime Minister. In those days, I would visit my professor, Dr Mishra, a philosopher and a great lover of books, in his simple two-room house. It was a bare house with no shelves, and so his books, covered with dust, were piled in every corner, much like wooden logs. Invariably, I would sneak some time out from the dry academic work to look at these, handling them with the same thrill I experienced as a child playing treasure-hunt games. It was here one day, in a forgotten book, that I found a picture of Neem Karoli Baba.

Memories flooded in. I was instantly transported to the early 1960s, when my mother and I would go on frequent visits to Kainchi, a small hamlet about 20 kilometres from Nainital, where Baba Maharaj had his ashram. As we would cross the wooden bridge over the Shipra river, the sounds of the Hare Rama kirtan would stream into our ears, mingled with the intermittent sound of bells accompanying the temple prayers. Hill women who had travelled from far in rickety buses, their heads covered decorously, would enter the ashram gates and first offer prayers at the temples on either side of the main courtyard, before making their way to Maharaj ji.

It was a familiar sight to see Maharaj ji seated on his takhat, in the verandah next to the Vindhyavasini Temple, surrounded by his devotees. This motley group included seekers who had come from the West and who now wore Indian clothes. The 1960s, after all, was the time when, attracted by the Indian concept of sanyaas, a huge mass of Westerners came to India in search of peace. Mixed up in this gathering were high-ranking officers, politicians, local women and rosy-cheeked children waiting for apples to be tossed to them by Maharaj ji. Questions were asked, and, many a time, answers were given even before the question was put forth. Blessings were sought and boons were bestowed.

Dressed in a simple white dhoti, with a blanket or a cotton sheet for a wrap-around, Maharaj ji shunned any insignia which would set him apart as a saint or a sadhu. Many a time, as he reclined on his takhat, visitors would walk up to him and ask where they could meet Neem Karoli Baba. His simple reply used to be, 'Main koi Baba ko nahi janta. Hanuman ji ke mandir me unse prarthna karo.' (I do not know any Baba! Go to the Hanuman Temple and pray to him.) On other occasions, he would loudly proclaim, 'Main kuch nahi janta.

Main toh prasad vala Baba hoon.' (I do not know anything. I am the Baba who gives prasad!)

Baba Neem Karoli, also known as Baba Neeb Karauri, was perhaps the most elusive embodiment of divinity in human form. Accepted and revered as the incarnation of Sri Hanuman, the son of Pawan—the god of wind—Maharaj ji too had the attributes of the wind. Sometimes he could be a gentle soothing whiff; at other times, a hurricane, a whirlwind. But always the bestower of life-giving breath. Nothing could bind him, no one could define him. As we devotees believe, he had no beginning, he *has* no end. 'There can be no biography of him', wrote his devotee Anjani in the blurb of his renowned disciple Ram Dass's[1] book *Miracle of Love*. 'Facts are few, stories many. He seems to have been known by different names in many parts of India, appearing and disappearing through the years.'

Named Lakshmi Narayan at birth, in the early 1900s, Maharaj ji left his native village of Akbarpur in Uttar Pradesh as a wandering sadhu when he was only eleven years old. As he travelled to various parts of India, he came to be known by different names. For instance, he was known as Tallaia-wale Baba in Gujarat. This was because in Babania he was seen performing spiritual sadhana by the waters of a small lake. The women of the village, with brass pitchers on their heads and veils drawn over their faces, would go to the lake to draw water and would often spot a young mendicant on the shore.

---

[1] Dr Richard Alpert, former professor of psychology at Harvard University, was later given the name Ram Dass by Maharaj ji.

On seeing them, Baba would dive into the water and remain submerged for prolonged periods.

Also known as Tikonia-wale Baba and Handi-wale Baba over the years, Maharaj ji then returned home to lead a householder's life for a few years, after which he left home again. Later, he was known as Baba Lachman Dass in the remote areas of western Uttar Pradesh. Eventually, after his stay in the village of Neem Karoli, he came to be known as Neem Karoli Baba. No one can tell which way the wind blew—but it appears that in the 1940s, from the plains of Uttar Pradesh, Maharaj ji proceeded to the mountains of Kumaon. And with his arrival, the hills began to soon be dotted with Hanuman temples.

An oft-asked question is: who was Neem Karoli Baba? Was he a mystic, an ascetic who aspired for and achieved the highest powers, the siddhis? Was he one of those miracle-sadhus so abundant in India? Or just a grandfather-figure in the homes he visited, fondly called 'Hanuman buju' by the children of Kumaon? These varied questions perhaps have varied answers, for Maharaj ji excelled in the art of deluding aspirants the moment they got a glimpse of even a tiny ray of his infinite spiritual depth.

If put to me, this question would have a simple answer: Maharaj ji was divine love incarnate.

I remember hearing this anecdote. One day, sitting in a gathering, he suddenly turned to ask an elderly lady: 'Tum mujhko kyon pyaar karte ho?' (Why do you have such love for me?) And then, before the baffled person could think of an appropriate reply, he himself answered, 'Kyon ki main tumko pyaar karta hoon.' (Because I have such love for you.) His love was beyond the law of cause and effect. The incessant flow of his grace and compassion seemed to have had no reason and no season.

My darshans of Maharaj ji were limited to a dozen or more times, when I visited the ashram in Kainchi with my mother in my younger days. At the time, the ashram comprised a few small temples and modest 'kutis'[2] with one or two rooms. While on most of these occasions I remember Maharaj ji seated on the takhat in the verandah, sometimes we would be told that he was in the woods nearby. Mummy and I would then walk up a hill and find him sitting under a tree, on a bed of wild grass, his coarse blanket carelessly draped around his shoulders. He would always greet us with questions: 'Kahaan se aaye? Kaun kaun aaya?' (Where have you come from? Who all have come?)

One specific incident is still vivid in my mind. It was raining that day and we reached Kainchi late. At that time, we were still unfamiliar with the mores of the ashram. We were told that there would be no audience today, since Maharaj ji's bhog had been taken to his kuti and offered to him. Though disappointed, we accepted this and started walking towards the temples. Soon, a messenger came running. 'Maharaj ji is calling you!" he said. Mummy and I quickly followed him, and he led us to the kuti. Maharaj ji was sitting on the takhat, and his bhog thali was placed in front of him. Smiling, he pushed the

---

[2] A little hut; usually ascetics live in these.

thali towards us and told us to eat the prasad. Mummy was initially hesitant to eat in front of Maharaj ji, but with great affection he insisted that we must eat then and there. As I sat quietly beside my mother, with no idea of what a great blessing had been conferred upon us that day, Maharaj ji ruffled my hair and asked, 'Yeh kiski ladki hai?' (Whose child is this?)

To explain this cryptic question that Maharaj ji posed, I have to go further back in time, to the day Neem Karoli Baba came into our lives.

*

My family usually spent the months of May, June and July in Nainital, at our house there. The summer I was seven years old, I remember we were having dinner at Prasada Bhawan one evening. I can still recall vividly the ivory walls and the wine-red carpet of the dining room. At the head of the table sat my Nana ji, who was visiting, my mother and father on either side of him, after which came the next generation. As the youngest, my chair was at the very end of the table. At around 8 p.m. or so, my mother, who faced the entrance hall, suddenly got up from her chair, saying, 'Baba Neem Karoli has come!' Her knife and fork clattered onto the dining table as she rushed towards the portico. All of us followed her, but there was no one there. My mother continued to insist that she had seen Maharaj ji enter through the main door. My father began to tease her playfully. 'Now that you've started seeing visions of saints, you've become a saint yourself!'

After a little laughter, we resumed dinner. Things went on as usual.

The next day, a telephone call came from the Commissioner's residence, informing us that Baba Neem Karoli would be visiting our house. In fact, we were told, he was already on his way! This came as a complete surprise as no one in the family was his devotee, even though Nana ji and Mummy had met him earlier at Bhoomiadhaar, close to Nainital. We were a traditional Hindu family. We observed all Hindu festivals—the Bhagavad Gita and worship of the Devi were of particular importance—but my father was averse to sadhus and ashrams. Mummy, on the other hand, would visit temples and pay homage to saints and sages she came to know about.

When we got the news that Maharaj ji was coming, I observed everyone's reactions the way all children do, without judgement. My father wasted no time in announcing that he could touch a poor man's feet, but he would not bow down to any Baba. Mummy, trying in her own way to convince him to offer pranaam to Maharaj ji, got busy getting some halwa made for prasad.

Soon enough, Maharaj ji's jeep stopped at our gate. We saw him almost jump out of the vehicle, and he started walking up the steep gravel path leading up to the house, accompanied by a group of people. I still remember how briskly Maharaj ji walked, barefoot, an arresting figure in a dhoti and kambal. My parents were standing at the portico to receive him. There was some excitement in the air as to how my father would greet him. But within moments, he walked straight ahead and touched Maharaj ji's feet. We all followed him.

Afterwards, Maharaj ji went into the drawing room and reclined on the sofa. I just have to close my eyes and I can see that sofa—it was beige, dotted with maroon chinar leaves—and Maharaj ji reclining on it. One of his devotees, who was sitting near his feet, entered a state of samaadhi. This was followed by a brief silence.

Then my father said, 'Baba, aaj bahut dinon baad aap ko dekha.' (Baba, today I am seeing you after a long time.)

This was a little unexpected. We were all taken by surprise at this.

Maharaj ji replied, 'Kyon, kal raat toh main yahaan aaya thha . . . kou ne na dekha.' He pointed to Mummy, 'Tai ne dekha.' (Why, I came here last night . . . No one saw me. *She* saw me.)

We were stunned because Mummy had indeed seen him the night before.

Turning to my father, Maharaj ji asked him, 'Tai ne mujhe kab dekha?' (When did you see me?)

We watched in bewilderment as my father replied, 'Baba, maine aapko 1933 mein dekha. Aapne meri raksha kari. Main Aligarh Muslim University mein padhta tha. Mere doston ne ek mor maar daala. Vahaan ke gaon wale dande le kar humko maarne daude. Hum sab bhaage, magar main pichhe rah gaya. Paas me ek mandir thha. Aap vahaan khade thhey. Aapne mandir ka darwaaza khol ke mujhe andar chhipa diya aur gaon waale aage nikal gaye.' (Baba, I saw you in 1933. I was studying at the Aligarh Muslim University. My friends killed a peacock. The enraged villagers chased us with sticks. All of us tried to flee but I got left behind. There was a temple nearby. You were standing there. You opened the temple door and hid me inside. The villagers went ahead.)

After this conversation, Maharaj ji was offered halwa-prasad and fruit, which he happily distributed to all those present. This was followed by tea, so the gathering shifted to the dining room. Maharaj ji then got up and went into the glazed verandah (now the library) on one side of the house. My mother followed him, and I followed my mother. We sat on the floor close to Maharaj ji. He spoke to Mummy about my father's diabetes, which none of us had mentioned to him. Commending Mummy on her piety, he ran his fingers through my hair in a playful way. Smiling, he told her, 'Yeh meri ladki hai.' (This child is mine.)

This was the answer to the question he used to ask me every time I went to Kainchi after that.

*

In later years, when I was living with Sri Siddhi Ma in Kainchi, I often asked her why Maharaj ji had visited our house that summer as none of us were his devotees then. For me, it was now distressing to look back and see Maharaj ji walking barefoot on the pebbled path. We had not welcomed him in the traditional way, with arati and puja as is normally done, no separate asana had been provided for him . . . we were just very,

very happy he had come. So, again and again I would ask her, 'Ma, why did he come?'

First, her silence. Then her beautiful smile. And finally the words, 'Tere liye aye.'

He came for you.

Chapter 2

At the turn of the twentieth century, the quaint little town of Almora, in what was then the United Provinces, was still pristine, unblemished by the strides of colonial modernity that had influenced other similar towns in the Himalayas, those particularly neighbouring Nainital. Well-known as a centre for cultural practice and reformist zeal, Almora also had a deep and ancient spiritual heritage. This is evident from the temples that adorn this Himalayan town, the most prominent being the nine mandirs dedicated to the worship of the Devi, eight to Bhairav Nath, a manifestation of Lord Shiva, and the Katarmal Surya Temple, which is one of the famous sun temples of India.

The spiritual energy of this town was further churned by the visits of enlightened souls. Swami Vivekananda wrote that after his return from Chicago and subsequent travels, his mind yearned for solitude, peace and quiet. It was then that he came to Almora, where he had the highest meditative experience. Nearly four decades later, in 1928, Monika Devi, the wife of Gyanendra Nath Chakravarty, the vice chancellor of Lucknow

University, became an ascetic and founded the Mirtola Ashram, 8 kilometres from Almora. She rose to be another spiritual luminary in the region, by the name of Yashoda Ma, and was eventually joined by her mystic disciple Swami Krishna Prem, formerly Ronald Henry Nixon, who had been a fighter pilot in the First World War. In 1937, Ma Anandamayee came to Almora en route to Mount Kailash, and said of this place: 'I see . . . that sadhus in astral bodies with matted hair are coming from within the ground and moving away . . . This proves that this is a place of penance.'[1] Perhaps this was the pull that brought various sadhus and mahatmas to Almora through the ages.

One day, in the mid-1930s, the locals who were bustling around the bazaar in Almora were taken by surprise when a tall figure clad in a blanket and dhoti suddenly appeared at a grocery store owned by Sri Pyare Lal Sah. What they didn't know was that Sri Sah's seven-year-old daughter, little Siddhi, who spent most of her free time there, was the one Baba had come to bless. In time, she would grow to be Neem Karoli Baba's prime disciple.

According to the Hindu belief system, the role of the guru is paramount in a seeker's life. The guru and the disciple are bound by a deep spiritual bond, which transcends the cycle of birth and death, and carries on from one life to the next. It is believed that when great masters incarnate, they bring with them their past disciples, and in a moment of divine transmission, the soul bond of many lives is rekindled. Perhaps this is what happened when Maharaj blessed Ma on that day, and the flame

---

[1]   http://www.shreeshreeanandamayeesangha.org/almora.html

was lit within. After this, Ma returned to the usual rhythm of her life. Maharaj wandered away into the mountains.

It was in the early 1940s when Baba Maharaj appeared on the horizon of Nainital again. He ushered in a devotional wave of Hanuman bhakti and the hills of Kumaon began to reverberate with the chanting of the Hanuman Chalisa and the Tulsi Ramayana, particularly the Sunder Kand, which relates how Hanuman ji went to Lanka in search of Ma Sita. In the years that followed, temples and ashrams in Hanumangarh,[2] Kainchi, Bhoomiadhar and Kaakrighat came up, and soon Maharaj ji became the spiritual father figure of almost every household in the region.

*

Sri Siddhi Ma was born in 1928, in Almora, on the tenth day of the Chaitra Navratri, to Sri Sah and Srimati Revati Devi. It is believed that the Sahs had originally been the treasurers of the Chand Dynasty, which had shifted its capital to Almora in 1563. According to Ma's horoscope, the date of birth was

---

[2] Hanumangarh Temple in Nainital: Maharaj ji had a small Hanuman murti installed in 1952. The main Hanuman Temple was consecrated on 16 June 1953. In later years, as the temple grew, more deities were added.

Kainchi Ashram, 19 kilometres from Nainital. How the forested place became the ashram is recounted later in the chapter.

Bhoomiadhar Temple, 11 kilometres from Nainital: The murti of Hanuman ji was installed in 1962.

Kaakrighat, 22 kilometres from Kainchi: The temple was consecrated in 1965.

31 March. At her naamkaran ceremony on the eleventh day, she was given the name Haripriya, but her father called her Siddhi. The favourite child of her father, amongst seven sisters, she loved spending time with him and helped in the shop after school hours. Even after many years, Ma would remember the colourful, foil-wrapped chocolates displayed in glass jars, which sometimes her father gave to her as a special treat. The family, while not affluent, never wanted for anything and a feeling of deep contentment prevailed in the household.

The Sahs lived in a traditional house in Khazanchi Mohalla, a narrow, low-roofed building, with a cluster of rooms, fairly small in size, with a beautifully carved wooden facade in those days. These Kumaoni houses were constructed with locally sourced material, including wood, stone and cow dung, and were plastered with mud. The sloping roof was made in four layers, with logs of pine, mud and slate tiles. The ground floor had a cowshed, with a low ceiling and small windows, which also served as storage for firewood. It was built in a sustainable way that insulated the entire structure, keeping it warm in the long winters. Ma reminisced in her later years, that because of the warmth, the barn would be her chosen place to play when she was a child on cold winter evenings. There was no electricity and so they used kerosene lanterns and oil wick lamps in the evenings. The one great luxury was a tap that provided running water.

As a child, her hair braided neatly, Ma wore pahaadi pyjamas, a shirt and a cotton topi, and was often taken for a little boy. In those days, it was customary in the hills for the little girls to be dressed often like little boys, in small coats and woollen trousers to keep them warm. (Three decades later, in the ashram in Kainchi, Maharaj ji would smilingly remind Ma about the clothes she'd worn when he first saw her.)

Ma's day at home would begin with a bath, after which all the children were supposed to write Ram Ram in their wooden slates. The previous night, they would have polished the slates and kept them ready, and now they wrote the lord's name with pens made of reeds, that were dipped in chalk solution before writing. The sisters would compete with one another to establish who wrote the best. After this, they would joyfully recite the Hanuman Chalisa and take a sip of Gangajal. Only after this would they eat breakfast and run to school.

After classes were over for the day, Ma would rush to her father's shop. Late afternoon, when the shops in the bazaar would close, their patios served as playrooms for the children of the neighbourhood. Her maternal grandfather had a godown for quilts and mattresses, which served as a perfect spot for hide and seek. At other times, she would play 'stapu' or hopscotch with the other children in the cobbled streets. Another game Ma excelled at was 'gitte', played with five small pieces of stone that were expertly tossed in the air and picked up from the ground in different permutations and combinations.[3]

---

[3] In later years, I had myself observed that while resting in the woods during her walks, Ma would pick pebbles that might be lying around and spontaneously start playing gitte. Her fingers moved deftly as she caught the pebbles one by one, her expertise apparent! I must confess that when she would ask me to play, I would never manage the gitte!

Barely eight years of age, her daily evening routine was to go to the nearby temples in time for the evening arati. Her little friend Lakshmi would join her in the narrow passage just below the house, and secretly the two would hold hands and go from temple to temple, to ring the bells and bring prasad for their mothers. The prasad was usually a few sugar crystals or one or two small pieces of coconut. At home too, there was a small niche in the wall in which Ma had kept a picture of Sri Radha and Sri Krishna. It was a passion with her to decorate this little altar. When flower-sellers came to their street, Ma would run down to them and buy flowers. In fact, sweet peas—what she called 'matar wale phool'—remained her favourite and every year she would wait for their season.[4]

Ma's favourite temple was the Raghunath Mandir of Almora, a deeply spiritual spot where Swami Vivekananda is also said to have meditated. She would tiptoe in, and evading the eye of the priest, sit on the lap of Lord Ganesha. While narrating this story to me, Ma would smile and say, 'Main kitni chhoti rahin hoongi, jo Ganesh ji ki godi me baith jaati thhi!' (How small must I have been to be able to sit in Ganesh ji's lap!) It is interesting to note that Siddhi is also the name of one of the wives of Ganesh ji.

---

[4] This love of arranging flowers continued to the Kainchi days, as we shall see later. After her daily morning round of the ashram, Ma would pick out flowers, mostly roses and green honeysuckle creepers, and arrange these flowers in Maharaj ji's kuti and by his takhat. The joy of doing this would be evident on her face.

The Uttarayani Fair is generally held in the second week of January every year on Makar Sankranti, and in Kumaon, the most famous one was held in Bageshwar on the banks of the Saryu river. Ma remembered going to the mela with her uncle. A part of the journey was by bus, a part on foot, all their wares loaded onto a mule. Sometimes, Ma's little feet would get tired, so her uncle would hire another mule for her to ride on. Even though a child, Ma would help her uncle out as he traded his wares.

On the first day of Chaitra came the festival of Phooldei. The little girls of the neighbourhood would get together and pick the fresh blooms of rhododendron. Ma particularly enjoyed this ritual. They would go from door to door in a group and shower these flowers and a few grains of rice on the threshold of each house in the neighbourhood, invoking auspiciousness upon the household. In return, the children would get rice, pieces of jaggery and blessings.

By the time Ma was ten or eleven, she would lead a group of children and enact a performance of the Ram Lila or Krishna Lila during the holidays. The venue would be either the courtyard of the Murli Manohar Temple or an open space at the back of the house where she lived. Ma was usually the director of the play but sometimes, being taller than the other children of her age, she would enact the role of Sri Ram or Sri Krishna. During periods of drought, the elders would gather the children and ask them to pray for rain. Under the leadership of our little Ma, her playmates—both Hindu and Muslim children—would form a group and march up and down the street in the bazaar. They would look up at the sky and loudly chant:

Allah miya paani de,
Paani de, gud dani de,
Paani gaya khet mein,
Roti gayi pet mein

(Allah give us rain. Rain will water the fields. We will get food to eat. And also sweet treats.[5])

In time, it would rain.

*

Down the hill from Ma's house was a modest hut with a slate roof. Here lived an old woman, Kaushalya. She had a cow and sold milk to make a small living. Ma's affections for the old lady—whom she called Kaushalya Amma—were perhaps the result of a bond from another life. Once, while driving through Almora, Ma pointed to a slope in Dharanaula, and told me that she would go there with Kaushalya Amma, to help her cut grass for her cow and collect wood for her stove.

Amma would cook food for herself on a wood fire and, before eating, she would save a portion of it for Ma. On her way back from school, Ma would run down to the hut and eat the food kept for her there. Rice and wheat were unaffordable luxuries for Amma, so it was usually coarse hill-grains, like madira and madua. The roti would be eaten with milk or

---

[5] This is an approximation and not a line-by-line translation.

curd. Often, Ma would also stay the night in Amma's hut. The bedding was just two coarse black blankets, one to spread on the mud floor, and the other to use as a cover. (This turned into a preference for coarse black blankets that lasted Ma a lifetime.)

In later years, when Ma was visiting her mother in Almora, one day she got an urgent message to return to Nainital. It was a Saturday, considered a very inauspicious day for undertaking a journey, but such was the seriousness of the summons that Ma was compelled to leave. When Kaushalya Amma came to know that Ma had to leave Almora on a Saturday, she was convinced in her heart that some great misfortune had befallen Ma. Unable to bear the agony of this, she left her body the same day.

In 1990, when Ma went on a pilgrimage to Gaya, she herself performed the shraadh for Kaushalya Amma on the banks of the Phalgu river. In this, she transcended the norms of her spiritual life to perform this ritual, since Kaushalya Amma had no one of her own to do it for her.

*

In the year 1944, at the age of sixteen, Ma was married to Sri Tularam Sah, a well-known advocate from Nainital. His large joint family lived in Tallital at the time.

One morning, the word spread that Maharaj ji was visiting the house of Sri Ram Sah, a local businessman. The ladies in Ma's family decided to go for his darshan. Ma went with them.

Ma in Kainchi in her early years

It was customary in those days for brides to maintain a certain restraint in their behaviour, and perhaps it was for this reason that Ma sat at the very back of the hall.

Baba was surrounded by a large group of devotees. Seeing Ma, he pointed his finger towards her and gestured for her to come forward. Ma came up close and offered pranaam. Maharaj ji immediately went on to give a vivid account of Ma's silent sadhana to the gathering, the constant flow of Ram's name with each breath she took, her high meditative state, and how she lived her life in the world like 'a lotus in water, yet above the water'. Then he made the prophetic statement, loud enough for all to hear, that he would make a kuti for her in Vrindavan. Considering this to be a foreboding of renunciation, of leaving this worldly life for a higher spiritual calling, thoughts of uncertainty regarding Ma's future crossed the minds of elders who were present there.

Shortly after, in 1947, the India Hotel was established by the family, and they changed their residence to Gita Bhavan, a house which was located just above the hotel. Very soon, Gita Bhavan became a venue for spiritual gatherings among the ladies of Nainital. Continuous chanting of the *Ramayana*, celebrations on Krishna Janmashtami, kirtan on every Poornamasi (full moon) day, and the daily ritual of arati in her small temple every morning and evening: it all added to the devotional hue of Nainital. Around this time, Ma also began to attend spiritual discourses given by Haridas Baba, Anandamayee Ma, Swami Vidyanand ji and other renowned saints who visited Nainital. In time, it became a practice for all devotees going to Kailash Mansarovar to commence their holy pilgrimage by first going for Ma's darshan. They would partake of the prasad offered to them at Gita Bhavan, and Ma would thoughtfully provide the pilgrims with blankets, warm woollen sweaters and other requisites for the hazardous journey.

With the building of the Hanumangarh Temple on Manora Hill in 1952, Maharaj ji's visits to Nainital became more frequent. In those years, on some days he would give darshan to Ma at Gita Bhavan. When he was in Hanumangarh, Ma would walk the 2 kilometres to the temple every day. Since Ma had household responsibilities, she would leave home as early as 2 a.m. in order to receive his darshan at dawn. Maharaj ji would be sitting on his takhat in his small kuti atop the hill,

Sri Siddhi Ma

wrapped in a blanket, with one or two devotees. A kerosene lantern would be burning in the corner. Often Maharaj ji would ask Ma to sing a bhajan. Ma had a deep sonorous voice. Baba's two favourite bhajans, she told me, were 'Ho nirvikar tathapi tum . . .' and 'Sumiran kar le mere mana'. All the while she sat there and sang with her eyes closed, tears flowed from Maharaj ji's eyes.

Over the years Ma's family went with Maharaj ji on pilgrimages to various shrines and temples in India: Rameshwaram, Jagannath Puri, Badrinath, Balaji Tirupati, Prayag, and so on. Usually, arrangements would be made for their stay in dharamshalas. For instance, I remember Ma telling me that they would stay at the 'Doodh-wali dharamshala' in Puri or the Sindhi dharamshala in Chennai.

In 1962, Tularam ji passed away. A year later, Ma, accompanied by Jivanti Mataji, began to live in the ashram at Kainchi.

*

Maharaj ji had first visited Kainchi with Ma in the early 1960s. At the time, it was so densely forested that sunlight would not filter through the foliage and reach the ground. The villagers were afraid to go there, even in the daytime, because of wild animals, mainly leopards, porcupines and barking deer. The Shipra river flowed past the forest, and on the other bank there were a few modest houses with slate roofs, made of stone and plastered with clay.

One day, Maharaj ji was returning to Nainital from Ranikhet, accompanied by Ma. There had been a bereavement in Ma's family. On the way, Maharaj ji told the driver to stop the jeep on the main road. Ma helped him cross the river and they entered the forests on the other side. There was a huge rock under an uttees tree. Maharaj ji said he would remain there, sitting on the rock, and asked Ma to proceed to Nainital. On her way back to the vehicle, Ma asked a local man the name of the place. He replied, 'Kainchi'. That was her first initiation to the place that was to become her spiritual sanctuary for decades.

The rock where Maharaj ji sat that day is now known as 'Maharaj ji's shila'. It is a place of prayer for all of us. The river in Kainchi incidentally flows northwards, something which is regarded as auspicious, and it was given the name 'Uttarvahini Ganga' by Maharaj ji. Perhaps the reason for Baba to select Kainchi was that the place had been sanctified by many saints who had lived or meditated there in earlier years. Somvar Giri Baba,[6] an enlightened sage, would invariably make a stop in a rock cave in Kainchi, on his way to Padam Puri or Kakrighat. This small cave located behind the Hanuman Temple in the ashram has been preserved as it was. On clearing the land, the havan kund where Somvar Giri Baba performed oblations in the fire was also found. In the early 1950s, a sage known as Kamla Giri Baba lived here too, and organized readings of the *Shiva Purana* and the *Devi Bhagwata*. Another name often mentioned in this context is that of Premi Baba, who used to live in a hut in Kainchi village.

To the east of Kainchi is the towering Gargachal range and it takes its name from Garga Rishi, preceptor of Sri Krishna, who is said to have performed spiritual austerities here. Years later, when I had begun to live in Kainchi myself—on some sunny days—Ma would draw my attention to a length of saffron or white cloth fluttering away on the peak of Gargachal, vivid against the blue skies, clearly at an elevation where there

---

[6] Born in Pind Dadan Khan, a city in the Jhelum district of Punjab, now in Pakistan, he left home at the age of twelve and proceeded towards the mountains of Uttarakhand where he did intense saadhna and attained enlightenment. He chose Padampuri and Kakrighat as his tapasthali (place of meditation). In Kakrighat, he had a small kuti and a dhuni under the banyan tree. Next to the kuti was the Shivaling worshipped by him. Every Monday there would be a 'khichdi' bhandara, and Baba was known for this as 'Somvari' or Somvar Giri Baba.

was no human habitation. Sometimes at night, we would see a huge beam of light radiating down from the mountaintop. While performing arati in Maharaj ji's kuti in the ashram, Ma would tell me to offer arati to this hill as well, where, she said, many siddhas still lived.

Chapter 3

The day Ma had Maharaj ji's darshan in the house of Sri Ram Sah in Nainital, that very same day there was another divine soul in the gathering who also received her first darshan of him. This was Sri Jivanti Mataji, who in the years ahead came to be a part of Ma and Maharaj ji's leela. After waiting for her turn patiently in that crowded room, when she bent down at Maharaj ji's feet to offer pranaam, he blessed her and said, 'Badi sant hai, badi sant hai! Hame roti khilayegi.' (She is very saintly, very saintly. She will feed me one day.)

These turned out to be prescient words. Years later in Kainchi, it was Jivanti Mataji—or Chhoti Ma as she was called in the ashram[1]—who cooked prasad for Maharaj ji every day. A small room above the office in Kainchi was her improvised kitchen, and she was often seen going up and down the temple courtyard, carrying prasad or hot water or milk for Maharaj ji.

---

[1] Though older in years to Ma, Jivanti Mataji was fondly known in Kainchi as Chhoti Ma (or Nan Ma in Kumaoni). This was to emphasize Ma's higher spiritual position.

With much affection, Maharaj ji would address her as 'Jivanti Lalli', lalli being a term of endearment for a beloved daughter.

Born in a Brahmin family in Almora, Jivanti Ma was married when she was still a child. As destiny would have it, the boy to whom she was married, Narayan Pant, succumbed to an illness and died young. Her parents passed away soon after, and Jivanti Ma was subsequently brought up by her widowed grandmother. Deeply religious and a renunciate by nature, she was thus freed from the bondage of worldly ties and unfettered to follow the spiritual path. To make ends meet, she worked as a primary-school teacher in Nainital and earned the princely sum of sixteen rupees a month from teaching.

In Nainital, on her way to school in the mornings, Jivanti Mataji would see Ma walking on the other side of the road, on her way to the Naina Devi Temple. They had seen each other at Sri Ram Sah's house, and Jivanti Ma was attracted to Ma's graceful and saintly demeanour. In Jivanti Mataji's words, 'Main unko roz dekhti thhi. Ma bahut halke rang ke kapde pahenti thhi. Apne dhyaan me chalti thhi. Unka mann kahin door rahta thha.' (I would see her every day. Ma would wear pastel-coloured clothes. Even while walking, she seemed to be in a meditative state. Her thoughts were somewhere far away.)

One day in the late 1950s, Jivanti Mataji visited Ma at home, accompanied by a colleague. Ma was in her kitchen, and she invited them inside. In Kainchi, Jivanti Mataji would later recall the scene to me. The kitchen floor was plastered with clay. Well-scrubbed utensils were neatly stacked on one side. Ma was sitting on the floor, cooking on a wood fire. Observing the naturalness of Ma's manner and the purity of the food being cooked, Jivanti Mataji had an irresistible desire to partake of the prasad. This was a surprise to Chhoti Ma herself. For orthodox Brahmins, eating in the homes of people belonging to other communities was not permitted. However, when Ma asked her if she would like to have prasad, it did not take Jivanti Mataji a moment to set aside this life-long norm. She sat in the kitchen and ate the prasad which was served to her in a thali by Ma herself.

In those years, Chhoti Mataji lived in a set of two tiny rented rooms on the way to Hanumangarh. One room had her puja altar and the other was used for living purposes. After her classes in school were over, she would return home and quickly cook food, offer it as bhog to Maharaj ji's photograph, take prasad herself and then go for Maharaj ji's darshan. One day, Chhoti Ma cooked daal and roti but when she placed the bhog in front of Maharaj ji, she realized that the grains in the dal were not fully cooked. She quickly put the prasad thali aside. Keeping a plate full of fruit in front of Maharaj ji's photo, she left for Kainchi.

On reaching the ashram, she saw Maharaj ji sitting on his takhat, with a group of people surrounding him. As soon as Jivanti Mataji did pranaam, Maharaj ji started telling the gathering in a child-like way, 'Aaj isne mujhe prasad nahin khilaya! Isne mujhe bhookha rakhkha, isne mujhe bhookha rakhkha!' (She did not give me food today! She has kept me hungry, she has kept me hungry!) Though a little embarrassed since the gathering was large, Chhoti Mataji was also happy, taking this as a sign of his divine omniscience.

Once Maharaj ji did not give darshan to devotees in Nainital for a long time. It was decided then that they would get together and take turns to chant the *Ramayana* till Maharaj ji heard the call of their hearts and appeared in their midst. Jivanti Mataji's puja room at home, sacred and pure like the kuti of a sage in the days of yore, was chosen for the continuous *Ramayana* paath. The reading of the text would start every morning and the entire book would be completed in twenty-four hours. On completion, arati would be done in the mornings, and the next recitation would start. This went on for twenty-five days.

Jivanti Mataji tells us that at 11 p.m., on the twenty-fifth night, the door burst open. She looked up and they all

Sri Jivanti Mataji

saw Maharaj ji standing at the threshold, holding the doors open with both his hands. A wave of joy engulfed the room. Jivanti Mataji placed the *Ramayana* in his hands, and arati was performed to Maharaj ji, and there was a great hustle-bustle around him. Everybody wanted to get close to him, offer pranaam, and within moments it became very festive. Baba stayed on for some time, took prasad himself and distributed it to everyone. Much later that night, he left for the Hanumangarh Temple.

Next morning, the news spread that Maharaj ji was in Hanumangarh, and large numbers of people began to stream in for his darshan. After meeting them, Maharaj ji told everyone to go to Jivanti Mataji's house as a bhandara[2] was happening there. Seeing the big crowd, some old devotees—who knew that Jivanti Mataji was a teacher in a primary school with limited means—expressed their concerns to Maharaj ji. How would she provide prasad to so many people? Maharaj ji waved aside their words. 'Tum nahi jante Jivanti Mai ko. Voh to Kuber ke bhandaar ki malik hai.' (You people don't know Jivanti Mai. She is the mistress of the treasure-house of Kuber, the god of wealth.)

When Jivanti Mataji was informed that Maharaj ji was sending people to her house for prasad, she asked a few ladies to carry out the necessary arrangements for the havan at her place, and herself hurried to the market to buy vegetables. She

---

[2] A bhandara is the ritual feeding of people at large. Anyone from anywhere can come into a bhandara and partake of the prasad. It is usually held on days of religious significance or the completion of a spiritual ceremony.

bought vegetables for 14 annas, and two-and-a-half kilos of ghee. People poured in throughout the day, and all were fed heartily from what seemed like a never-ending store of prasad.

*

In 1962, after the death of Ma's husband, Maharaj ji told Jivanti Mataji that from now onwards she should live with Ma. She resigned from her job at the school and lived with Ma for the next four decades, first in Nainital, and then in Kainchi.

In the ashram in Kainchi, it was Jivanti Mataji who decided the quantity of food to be cooked each following day. In the evenings, she would tell the kitchen staff how many kilos of puris were to be made in the ashram, and these would always be sufficient for visitors. Every morning, two steel buckets full of puris and potatoes would be placed on the takhat in the room adjacent to Maharaj ji's kuti. (Chhoti Ma was very particular that both of these be kept covered with leaf-plates.) For hours she would sit on a cane chair and pack this puri prasad from the buckets for those who came to the ashram. The supply of puris and potatoes always seemed endless.

Devotees who might be leaving Kainchi after darshan, to undertake long train journeys home, were given food prasad in cardboard boxes. The contents would normally be a few puris or chapattis, some vegetables and a small pouch of pickle. This was done by Chhoti Mataji herself. She would remember who was a diabetic and avoided putting a sweet in their box; if someone suffered from hypertension, their food would be without salt. People still remember the taste of that 'raaste ka prasad', and the way it was packed with such love and care by Chhoti Mataji's own hands.

In the ashram in Kainchi or wherever else they went, the mothers were always seen together. Ma, tall and slender, her head covered, and Jivanti Mataji, short and fair, wearing dark-rimmed spectacles. Both always wore white khadi dhotees, and sometimes in winter, a shawl or sweater. Theirs was a beautiful blending of two spiritual souls. Ma, so unworldly, so merged-in-Maharaj ji, and Jivanti Mataji, her guide and companion, so spiritually sanguine and intuitive. From the tiniest of decisions to the most vital, Ma looked up to Jivanti Mataji, and it was her word that prevailed. Today as I write this, I realize that what Ma was to Maharaj ji, Jivanti Mataji was to Ma.

Chapter 4

It was a pleasant day in July 1980. No sun, no rain. Just a cool breeze, clouds drifting in the sky, and a slight drizzle now and then. I was driving to Kainchi in my old Willy's jeep. With me were Mummy, her two friends and my four nephews—aged between seven and thirteen. Everyone was in a rather cheerful mood at the outing.

Baba Sri Neem Karoli Maharaj had left his mortal body seven years ago but Kainchi continued to have its own spiritual charm for us. On the way, as we traded memories of Maharaj ji, one of the ladies mentioned to my mother that there was a Mataji in the Kainchi temple now, who was Maharaj ji's prime disciple—would we like to have her darshan? My mother readily agreed but I remember saying airily, 'Not for me!'

Once we reached the ashram, after doing the usual rounds of the temples, the ladies proceeded for Mataji's darshan. I chose to stay with the boys by the river. They were running about, splashing in the water, being playful, and I was enjoying my time with them. Minutes later, a man came from inside and said that Mataji was calling me. Not really keen to go in, I used the pretext that the children could not be left alone by the river. After a little while came the temple pujari, Trilok Da, to say that Mataji wanted me to go in and have the lunch prasad. It didn't seem right to refuse again, and as it would be more appropriate for me to first offer my respects to Mataji before proceeding to eat, I asked Trilok Da to take me to her. The temple attendant offered to keep an eye on the boys.

I entered the little room and in front of me were two very serene elderly ladies wearing white dhotis, sitting on a mat which looked like a folded black blanket. Around them were seated five or six people, including members of our group. Seeing me, Ma smiled radiantly, and then stated, 'Yeh hai Jaya.' (This is Jaya.) It sounded like an acknowledgement rather than a question. I was confused. The joy on her face, the smile, the instant recognition—how could she be so happy to see someone who had been so disinclined to meet her?

I offered pranaam and took my place in the furthermost corner of the room.

Ma spoke; occasionally Chhoti Ma completed her sentences; everybody listened. The context of the conversation evaded me, but Ma's voice seemed to slowly permeate into my being. In a sudden moment of revelation, something within me said, 'Agar Krishan ki bansi hai, toh iss aawaaz me hai.' (If the sound of Krishna's flute is there anywhere, it is in this voice.)

By now the conversation had steered to the day Maharaj ji had come to Kainchi. Ma turned to me, 'Have you seen the rock on which Maharaj ji sat when he first came here?'

I said I had, but many years ago.

She said, 'Go and see it again.'

I did as I was told. Walking to the upper half of the ashram, I stood by Maharaj ji's shila. As I stood by the rock, enchanted by the tranquility of the spot, I closed my eyes for what must have been a moment or two. They seemed infinite though, merging my mind into a silent stillness I had never experienced before. The gentle caress of a hand on my head brought me back. I turned around and saw Ma standing behind me. I told her how peaceful it was. After a pause, she put her assuring hand upon my shoulder and said to me, 'Tu yahaan rahegi. Jahaan bhi dhyaan karegi, vahaan dhyaan lagega.' (You will live here. Wherever you want to meditate, you will be able to meditate.)

I was filled with confusion.

Meditate, yes. But live here? I'd had no such thoughts.

And yet, what *were* my thoughts?

The day was 21 July 1980, and ever since my father's passing in 1969 I had been on a silent spiritual quest for more than a decade. That deep yearning within, to find the meaning of life, had taken me to ashrams and sages across India. As a child I had met Swami Shivananda, and later I met his disciple Swami Chidananda, Anandamayee Ma, Deoraha Baba, and from 1970 onwards, Mummy and I spent several months each year in Sai Baba's ashram in Puttaparthi.

Even when I was young, beneath the joyous surface of my life—school and college, friends, the warmth of a loving family, holidays in India and abroad—there flowed within me a hidden stream that was almost compulsively searching for its source. With the exception of my mother, no one noticed this side of me though. Perhaps because there had never been any perceptive change in my lifestyle, and I was a part of all that went on at home and school with usual enthusiasm. As a family we were social, and there were lively luncheons for friends, and often formal dinners for dignitaries. There were regular visits by scholars such as Professor Nurul Hassan and Dr Girija Shankar Mishra, eminent personalities of the time such as Pandit Govind Vallabh Pant, Syed Ali Zaheer, Dr Sampoornanand, Keshav Dev Malviya, governors Dr Gopala Reddy and Dr Chenna Reddy, and several others, who all lent their hue to the gathering. Most days, I also enjoyed playing squash at the Balrampur estate next-door or badminton with friends at Hotel Metropole. Life went on as before, and the transition to the spiritual path was *so* gradual that it felt natural and came to be accepted as my chosen way of life by the family.

My Nanaji had a vast library of spiritual books in Chapslee, his house in Simla, and I was the only one in the family, other than him, who spent a great deal of time there, poring over these books. The publications of the Theosophical Society of India, the Ramakrishna Mission and the Bharatiya Vidya Bhavan, the books of Sri Aurobindo, Swami Vivekananda and Paramahamsa Yogananda, Paul Brunton's book that revealed Ramana Maharishi to the West, translations of the Vedas and the Upanishads that I handled but did not quite understand. On our way to Puttaparthi, it was a ritual to stop at the Vedanta Book House in Bangalore, where I would buy a stack of old books on the Himalayan yogis, who, somehow, inspired me deeply. I was in fact fortunate enough to meet a few of them on my trek to Gau Mukh, Kedarnath, which also took me to many lesser-known shrines hidden in the mountains.

But mostly, I read and read and read.

Now I realize that this too was part of the process. I was perhaps being prepared my whole life so I would be able to receive the spark when it came.

Ma walked back to the darshan room. I followed her. She told everyone that she had returned from Neem Karoli village a day earlier, and asked for the roti prasad from there to be brought to her. One of the ashram ladies fetched some rotis in a basket. Ma gave out one to each person in the room, except for me.

'You like reading books?' she asked me.

I was surprised that she should say this—it was, of course, entirely true. Ma picked up the last roti and kept it in her hands, turning it back and forth.

'Yes, Ma,' I said.

'Aaj se kitabein padhna chhod de', she said. (From today, stop reading.)

I was taken aback. But almost immediately after, I felt acceptance for this in my heart.

Now when I think back to that moment, I wonder why Ma had asked me to stop reading books. At the time, I read any and every book bordering on spirituality, whatever I got my hands on. Consequently, I was confused and not getting anywhere, anchorless—something like the proverbial rolling stone that gathers no moss. Perhaps the moment had come for Ma to

My early years with Ma

initiate me and set me on my final path; studying books of her choice was the first step.

Turning to the gathering, Ma quoted a bhajan: 'Parama divya, parama gopya, mantra Ram-naam.' (Deeply divine, precious secret, the mantra Ram-naam.) She went on to explain that Maharaj ji used to say, 'Raam-naam mein itni shakti hai ki vidhi ka likha anka bhi mit jaataa hai.' (Such is the power in the name of Ram that even what has been predetermined in our destiny can be rewritten!)

I took that as a message. The very next day I took my collection of spiritual books to Kainchi and left them in the small library there. It was time for me to set aside bookish knowledge and focus on meditating upon the lord's name.

Eventually we were all told to proceed for lunch, after which we would leave. I bowed down to offer pranaam. Placing the roti in my palms, Ma tenderly covered my hands with hers. She said, 'Main Jivanti se kah rahi thhi aaj jo aayegaa vo bada bhagyashaali hoga.' (I was telling Jivanti that whoever comes today will be very blessed.)

I was the last one to step out of the little room that day. Looking back at her, the revelation dawned on me that Ma was the one my soul had been searching for all these years.

I no longer wanted to leave.

*

In Nainital, spiritual programmes were often organized at the Govardhan Hall by the lake. One afternoon, three or four days after I met Ma for the first time at Kainchi, Mummy and I were going to attend one of these events. We were carrying with us a beautiful length of red velvet edged with gold for the altar at Govardhan Hall, where Maharaj ji's photograph was kept. It was just something that Mummy and I had wanted to do quietly as we had noticed that Maharaj ji's altar was looking very unkempt. We also gathered a few roses and other flowers from our garden.

As always, we were going to take my jeep, which was waiting by the porch.

I got in, turned the ignition, and shifted gears. Straight away the vehicle began to roll down the steep slope that led to and from Prasada Bhawan. As I tried to stop the jeep, I realized in a flash that the brakes were free. Mummy was sitting next to me and my instant decision was to ram the car into the horse chestnut tree that stood before the main gate, so as to avert a greater disaster.

The impact of the crash on the vehicle was intense. It got tossed up in the air and overturned. I was flung out, though my legs were pinned under the jeep. Mummy was still inside.

At that moment, I saw a clear vision of Ma, tall and serene in her white dhoti, towering over me.

The next second, there was commotion all around.

Almost magically, ten or so men came running in from the street. Together they lifted the vehicle and pulled me out first, and then rescued Mummy. All members of the household had come rushing out in the meantime. After the initial shock had waned, we discovered that Mummy only had a small scratch on her forehead, and I had a little pain in the upper back. We walked back to the house.

For hours after, my mind kept circling back to that moment when I was trapped under the jeep. I had been convinced that it was my time.

And then I saw Ma.

There could be no doubt any longer; Ma was here to save me.

Chapter 5

After that first meeting with Ma in Kainchi, it became hard to stay away. So, while the rest of my life seemed to be going on as usual—I would, in fact, be waking up as early at 3 a.m., getting ready in the dark, and nipping down to the garden to pick seasonal flowers for Ma in the torchlight—before driving to Kainchi. It would still be night outside when I'd leave home, the trees and mountains in shadow, and I would reach the ashram in the pristine silence of the morning.

Kainchi would just be waking up. The pujaris would be unlocking the temple doors, lighting the lamps, mopping the floors. My chosen place to wait while doing my japa[1] was a nook behind the Vindhyavasini Temple, facing Ma's blue window. I never had to wait long.

Soon I would hear a creak, and the shutter in front would be eased open. Ma would call out my name in her sweet voice and I would go closer, hands folded. Looking down at me from

---

[1] Ritual chanting of God's name or a mantra.

the window, a smile on her lips, she would speak to me. 'Itni jaldi aa gayee . . . Raat mein neend nahin aayee . . . Yeh trishna aisi hi hoti hai . . . Pyaasaa paani hi khojtaa hai . . . Main bhi jaldi doh baje Maharaj ji ki darshan ke liye Hanumangarh chali jaati thhi . . . magar jaldi lautnaa padta thha gharme kaam kaaj jo thhaa . . .' (You have come so early . . . Were you not able to sleep at night? . . . Yes, such is the longing . . . A thirsty person seeks nothing but water . . . I used to leave home as early as 2 a.m. and go to Hanumangarh for Maharaj ji's darshan . . . I had to be back early to attend to household work.)

After a short conversation, Ma would ask me to go home. The window would close.

On some days, Ma would open the corner door near the Devi Temple and quietly signal for me to come inside. This was Baba's kuti, his wooden bed on one side, a metal saggar smouldering in the corner, the scent of guggul permeating the room. I realized much later that this was a 'restricted zone' as very few were allowed in here. Ma would say, 'Yeh kuti Kainchi ka hriday hai.' (Maharaj ji's kuti is the heart of Kainchi.)

Eventually I got to learn from Ma that though Baba slept in the kuti across the courtyard at night—which was called the 'bahar wali kutiya' in Kainchi parlance, and which, for some reason, the Westerners called 'the office'—during the day he used to rest here. He would write 'Ram Ram' in a notebook, sitting on the wooden bed. A few of his close devotees would gather around him when he so desired, and he often asked one of them to read from the *Tulsi Ramayana*, the Bhagavad Gita or the *Gyaneshwari* of Samarth Ram Das. One of his favourites, in fact, was the book on the life of Sarada Devi, the consort of Sri Ramakrishna. Maharaj ji had a way of referring to the book as 'Jairambati', which was the birthplace of Ma Sarada.[2]

This kuti was where Maharaj ji passed on his spiritual legacy to Ma. A group of close devotees witnessed this extraordinary moment here, on 9 September 1973. It was mid-morning and Maharaj ji was writing 'Ram Ram' in his notebook, reclining on the takhat in his usual posture. While writing, he used to lean on the bed, resting on his elbow. That day, he wrote 'Ram Ram' for 9 and 10 September, and then after writing 11 September in the corner of the next page, slid the notebook across the takhat towards Ma, who had been sitting there, saying, 'Aaj se iss mein tu likhegi, Amma.' (From today, you will write in this, Amma.) The prophetic truth of those words dawned on those who were there when two days later, Maharaj ji took mahasamadhi in Vrindavan. Through the Ram Ram notebook, he had symbolically passed the sacred baton to Ma.

Until then, Sri Siddhi Ma had lived, from moment to moment, in service to the person of her guru. However, after she was bestowed the spiritual mantle, she gradually stepped out from the inner chambers of Kainchi. Now, along with Jivanti Mataji, she dedicated herself to serving Maharaj ji's ashrams and temples, enhancing their purity, and recreating them as havens where seekers would find their paths, and tired minds, escaping the upheavals of Kaliyuga, would find peace and tranquillity.

---

[2] These books are still kept in the shelves in Maharaj ji's kuti.

As we devotees believe, Neem Karoli Baba was an avatar of Hanuman ji himself. And when such souls grace the earth, it is the aura of their presence that blesses, teaches, gives and transforms in mysterious divine ways. To rationalize or analyse this phenomenon is beyond the ken of human intellect. In Maharaj ji's time, hundreds experienced this daily in his proximity. As Ma would say often, the Sanskrit word 'Upanishad' means 'being near'. When you are in the proximity of an enlightened saint, that is when transmission— and transformation—take place.

When Ram Dass came to Maharaj ji, he asked him how he could awaken his Kundalini shakti.[3] Maharaj ji tried to evade this first, suggesting he visit other sages. However, when Ram Dass persisted with the question, Maharaj ji finally said, 'Do akshar Ram-naam ke koi letaa nahin. Raam naam se asambhav bhi sambhav hotaa hai' (Two syllables, the name of Ram, no one wants to take! Even the impossible becomes possible with the name of Ram.)

This was the summum bonum of Maharaj ji's philosophy— the efficacy and power of the Lord's name. He would often give two examples. Valmiki, the robber, became a great sage and poet, and Hanuman ji crossed the ocean in one leap—all by taking the name of Ram.

In Maharaj ji's kuti, the most sacred place in Kainchi, I would spend a few precious minutes with Mother every

---

[3] The energy or 'shakti' which is believed to be located at the base of the spine, and when aroused, leads to spiritual awakening.

morning. Usually, Ma spoke, I listened. Sometimes, it was a story or two about Maharaj ji. Other times, it was spiritual guidance. For instance, even though earlier she had asked me to stop reading, she now began to give me books of her own choice. Some were abstruse, such as the *Ashtavakra Gita* or the *Yoga Vashishtha*, while others, like *The Gospel of Sri Ramakrishna* by M and *Commentaries on the Ramayana* by Ramkinkar ji were more accessible to me.

After about ten minutes or so, Ma would hurriedly get up and disappear inside. She would return with a shiny steel lota with tea in it. The fragrance of tulsi in the tea still lingers in my mind. Years later, I was deeply touched when I realised that Ma herself would make the tea for me on the coal-fire before my arrival, since the ashram kitchen opened much later.

Afterwards, Ma would ask me to return to Nainital. Often it was a one line goodbye: 'Jaa, ab toh mil gaye. Yeh kitne janmo ka hai.' (Go, now we have met. This is the bond of many lives.)

I would drive back home then, to my parallel life, in time for breakfast. The family would be at the dining table, my two elder brothers none the wiser about my morning pilgrimage.

*

Not long after, Ma began to ask me to stay in Kainchi for a few days at a time, so carrying a small suitcase and great joy in my heart, I would come to the ashram. When I think about these brief interludes, what I remember most vividly were the summer nights in Kainchi. The clear sky, the stars, the soft cool breeze, the fragrance of jasmine flowers that grew behind Maharaj ji's temple: it was enchanting. Past the midnight hour, when everyone slept, I would slip out of my room and go to the temples. I would sit in the silence and savour the sweetness of the night.

The night watchman would be in his cabin at the far end of the temple courtyard, sitting by a small fire, partially awake, partially asleep. The ashram dogs were tied in the verandah opposite Ma's room and sometimes they would bark at the slightest sound. Fearing that they would inadvertently end up disturbing Ma's sleep, I would try to quieten them down. As the night deepened, I would sit on the steps near Baba's takhat. Usually, between 2 a.m. and 3 a.m., Ma's window would slowly open. Sleepy-eyed, holding the window bars with both her hands, she would call out to me in a voice that was still husky with the remnants of sleep. To get closer to her, I would gently shift Baba's takhat, and kneel on the floor next to the window.

This would be my treasured time with Ma.

She would speak to me in small sentences, sharing reminiscences of her early life with Baba. 'Jaya', Ma would say, 'Maharaj ko mai ek bhajan sunati thhi, "Sumiran kar le mere mana, teri beeti umar Hari bhajan bina . . ." Baad mein, Maharaj mujhe "meri mana" kah kar pukaarte they . . .' (Jaya, I used to sing a devotional song for Maharaj, "Immerse the heart in the constant remembrance of the lord, my life has gone by without singing of the glories of Hari", and in later years, Maharaj used to call me "meri mana" from that.)

Talking of years when Ma was still at home, she would say that she had a long day full of household duties. As the youngest in the household in a large joint family, her responsibilities were many. Ma would, late at night, when the house had fallen silent, sit down to her sadhana. And time would lose its meaning for her. It would be in the wee hours of the morning that she would finally eat a little.

In later years, when Ma was living in Kainchi, she told me during one of these night-time conversations, that after offering the bhog thali to Maharaj ji in his kuti, she would wait by the takhat, in case he asked for something. On his thali, Maharaj ji would leave a small portion of the food he had partaken and unbeknownst to all except Chhoti Mataji, that is the sum of what Ma would eat that night.[4] This was maha prasad for Ma, and the true source of her spiritual energy.

Ma loved telling stories from the lives of saints and sages. One night, I remember, she spoke of the great saint Meera bai, how she had renounced the splendours of her royal palace and wandered the streets of Vrindavan singing the glories of Hari. Another night, she told me about Sakku bai, a great devotee of Lord Vitthal, who was tortured by her family members daily, until the Lord himself came to rescue her from her suffering. Ma said, 'Bhakti koi khel nahin . . . Lohe ke chane chabaane padte hai, talwar ki dhaar par chalnaa padta hai.' (Bhakti is no child's play. It's like chewing grains of steel, and walking on the

---

[4] Later in the book, we have talked at length about the spiritual importance of prasad to Maharaj ji and Ma.

sharp edge of a sword.) I asked, 'But Ma, why the suffering?'
She replied that pain and suffering strengthen sadhana, but so
intoxicated is the bhakta with love for god, that even thorns on
the path feel like petals.

Eknath, Tukaram, Namdev, Chokhamela: these great
Varkari saints from Maharashtra were her particular favourites,
and she liked to speak of their 'naam sadhana'. She said that
their way of bhakti was to chant the lord's name. 'Naam mein
badi bhari shakti hai, Jaya, naam hi sab kuchh hai. Isi se man
ekaagra hotaa hai', she would say. (The name has great power,
Jaya. It is the only way to focus the mind.) Telling me this, Ma
would softly sing a line from a devotional song, 'Prem mudit
man se kaho Ram Ram Ram . . . niraadhar ko aadhar ek Ram-
naam.' (With a heart full of love, sing Ram Ram Ram . . . the
only support of the helpless is the name of Ram.)

While speaking of Tukaram and the other Varkari saints,[5]
I observed that Ma was filled with an intense longing for the
darshan of Lord Vithoba of Pandharpur[6]—whom, she told me,

[5] Founded by great Bhakti saints like Dnyaneshwar, Tukaram, Namdev,
the Varkari movement was a part of the overall Bhakti movement
that was reforming religious orthodoxies in different parts of India. In
Maharashtra, the Varkaris made the idea of God accessible to people of
all castes and religions. Initiation into the Varkari path requires only three
things: opposition to narrow-minded religious practices, egalitarianism
in spiritual matters, and family-centred life.

[6] Pandharpur is a pilgrim town on the banks of the Chandrabhaga river,
in Solapur in Maharashtra, and is home to the famous Vithoba Temple.
Lord Vithoba—also called Vitthala or Panduranga—was worshipped by
the Varkari saints.

she had wanted to visit since she was a child of six. 'Jaya, mujhe Pandharpur le chal.' (Take me to Pandharpur, Jaya.) I would promptly reply, 'Ma, *aap* mujhko le jayengi.' (Ma, it is *you* who will take me.[7])

On those summer nights, Sri Ramakrishna and Sarada Ma would come up in conversation. Ma told me that upon the mention of Ramakrishna Paramhansa, Maharaj would smile at Ma, lift his forefinger to emphasise, and say, 'Guru chhi Guru chhi!' Guru thhey Guru thhey! What he meant in Pahaadi was that Sri Ramakrishna had been her guru in a past life.

One night, Ma came out of her room with a book in her hand and sat on the steps with me, near Maharaj ji's takhat, saying, 'Le yeh *Gita* tu rakh le . . . pehle mai iske bina rah nahi paati thhi', and she gave the book to me. (Keep this Gita with you . . . there was a time when I could not stay without it.) This Bhagavad Gita had been a constant companion for Ma when she lived in Nainital and this was the only possession she brought to the ashram with her. I was speechless that she thought me worthy of this precious prasad, and I received it from her with humble gratitude. Later, in Kainchi, I would sometimes bring the Gita to her, and clasping it in her hand,

---

[7] In 1994, Ma took me, along with several others, to Pandharpur, our final stop on a long pilgrimage to Dwarka. I can never forget the memory of the day as we waited for Lord Vithoba's darshan. Suddenly, I realized that Ma was not there with us. When we finally reached the sanctum sanctorum, we found that Ma was already there, standing before Lord Vithoba—her eyes closed, tears flowing, hands folded.

Ma would put it to her forehead and then, with eyes closed, she would embrace it.

During one of these summer nights a most extraordinary thing was revealed to me. Ma said, 'Did you know that when you were a baby, I used to see you every day? While walking to Govardhan Hall for satsang, I would see you near the Bandstand, wheeled by your ayah in a pram. I would stop to spend a moment with you.' I was amazed to hear this. Smiling, Ma went on to describe the frocks I wore, recalling the tiny roses embroidered on them, and even what my ayah wore— off-white khadi dhotis with large checks on them and long-sleeved woollen blouses.[8] The thought that Ma knew me so long before I 'knew' her was something that moved me very deeply, convincing me even more that my bond with her was from many lives ago.

When I think back to these night-time conversations with Ma, I can remember how it was for me—as though time would stop and the entire world would recede. There was just Ma.

And yet, there came a moment when I would realize that dawn was nigh and soon Kainchi would begin to awaken. Sensing that my time with Ma was coming to a close, I would pose to her the one question that was forever uppermost in my mind: *Will there ever come a day, Ma, when I will never have to leave you?*

---

[8] Ma called these waistcoat-like blouses 'salukas' in keeping with the tradition of the hills where they were commonly worn by the local women.

Ma would hold my hand through the window, and quote these lines spoken by Hanuman ji to Mother Sita from the 'Sunder Kaand' of the Tulsi Ramayan.

Kachuk divas janani dharu dhira,
Kapinh sahit aayinh Raghubira.[9]

---

[9] Here, Sri Hanuman ji pleads with Mother Sita to wait patiently for a few days, assuring her that Bhagwan Raghubir will come with his army of monkeys to take her.

Chapter 6

Gradually my stays in the ashram got longer and longer, months at a time. By mid 1980s, I was living in Kainchi. Till now, my time with Ma had been limited to either meeting her during the day in the darshan room, in a somewhat formal setting, or the few treasured moments with her at dawn and in the summer nights when I was staying at the ashram for short stretches. Now that I was in Kainchi all the time, little by little I got woven into the spiritual fabric of life in the ashram and I began to observe the minutiae of Ma's daily routine.

Ma would be out on the temple courtyard before the break of dawn. I would quietly watch her doing parikrama of Maharaj ji's temple, while it was still dark. Not wanting to disturb, I would stand at a distance as she circumambulated. A tall figure in white, barefoot, with a shawl carelessly draped around her shoulders, it was as though Ma was almost twirling around Maharaj ji's mandir, swiftly, lightly. Before the appearance of daylight, she would have visited all the temples. For many, this would be their first darshan of Ma that day. The devotees who lived in the ashram would be sitting in various corners, a few by the pillars, a few by Maharaj ji's takhat, immersed in their morning prayers, when Ma would stop by them and speak a word or two to each one. They would, in turn, offer their pranaams to her.

Afterwards, Ma would withdraw into the inner rooms of the ashram for a brief interlude. A lota of chai from the kitchen would be waiting for her and Chhoti Mataji in their kuti. Then Ma would take her bath. Immediately after, Ma would go to Maharaj ji's kuti.

Chhoti Mataji told me that once, years ago, Maharaj ji was sitting on his takhat and Ma, Jivanti Ma and a few other ladies were sitting on the floor around him. Ma wore her hair in a simple braid those days, and always kept her head covered with her dhoti. Maharaj ji slowly leaned over and unbraided Ma's hair. Since that day Ma never did her hair, nor did she use a comb herself. One or the other of the ashram ladies would comb her hair when the opportunity arose.

Inside Maharaj ji's kuti, Ma would spend a few minutes doing puja to a photograph of his feet. She would apply chandan[1] and kumkum[2], and then, she would place a single rose petal gently upon the toes. The little red petal, the way it was offered, and the expression on her face: every bit of

---

[1] Sandalwood paste.
[2] Vermilion powder.

this small gesture reflected the depth of her love. Soon after, Chhoti Mataji took over and continued the rest of the puja in Maharaj ji's kuti. During this time, Ma would sit in the verandah and arrange roses, along with honeysuckle creepers, in glass jars which were used as improvised vases. These would be placed in Baba's room, in front of his pictures. While arranging the flowers, Ma would also meet a few of the elderly ladies of the ashram and members of the staff, to gently guide them on specific things that had to be done in the ashram that day.

Time for the morning darshan nigh, Ma would make a quick round of the ashram kitchen. There, while rolling out puris, the ladies would be singing old traditional bhajans in their melodious voices. 'Dhanya dhanya Badri', they would sing sometimes, or 'Jagdamba Bhavani aayi mere angna'. At other times, it would be the Hanuman Chalisa or the repeated chanting of 'Sri Ram Jai Ram Jai Jai Ram'. Their voices would carry in the breeze and waft around the inner chambers of the ashram.

By now, people would have started congregating in the verandah outside the meeting room, and after partaking of a small bal bhog, both the mothers would proceed there. For the next few hours, that little darshan room was the hub of much activity, many comings, and goings. A few ladies would volunteer to organize the streams of visitors if it got very crowded. The two mothers would spend most of their morning here, meeting people. Sometimes a few devotees lingered till as late as 2:30 p.m., wishing to have more time with her, maybe even a one-on-one conversation, and only after the last devotee left would Ma withdraw inside.

*

In the ashram, after the food prasad had been offered in the temples, Ma and Chhoti Mataji's bhog was brought down to the Doodh Kaksh, once at mid-morning, around 11:30 a.m., and once at 7:30 p.m. in the evening. In this room, a square metal stove was kept, in which a fire burnt through the day, smouldering with round balls made of clay, cow dung and burnt coal. In Kainchi, this fuel is called 'guptol'. The steel containers that bore food for the mothers—originally from Maharaj ji's old hot-case—were placed on the embers to keep the food warm.

Ma had no set time to take her meals. It all depended on the devotees who wanted to meet her. Sometimes Chhoti Mataji, who might have left the darshan room to attend to other matters, would send a message to her via a few of us, asking Ma to come in and take lunch prasad. But to no avail. It was only after *all* had left that Ma would get up. Smiling, almost apologetically, she would say, 'Dekh toh, main kya karoon. Log itni door se Maharaj ji ke liye prem se aate hain, aane mein kasht sahte hain, itna paise kharachte hain. Unse mujhko milna padega.' (See, what can I do. People come from far and wide with love for Maharaj ji. They go through such difficulties and spend so much money to come here. I must meet them.)

By now, the time would be around 2:30 or 3 p.m. in the afternoon. Sometimes the rice would become brittle and the rotis, crisp and hard. Ma liked to mix everything in her thali together and then eat it. She liked curd, and she had a distinct fondness for sweets. She enjoyed the kheer made in the bhandara, sometimes the halwa prasad too. Occasionally she would ask for a small piece of jaggery after her meals, especially in the cold winter days. Ma's most favourite sweet, right from her childhood, was jalebi with dahi.

Together, the two mothers would savour the prasad in silence. After that, they were to retire to their kuti for an hour or so.

*

In the late afternoon, Chhoti Mataji and Ma would walk around the ashram, sit in the inner garden area or on the steps of the yagnashala. Many, seeking an opportunity to be around Ma, would gather nearby now. Some would help pick dry leaves in the garden, some might wash Maharaj ji's rock or clear weeds. Sometimes, the chosen spot would be by the perennial spring at the back of the ashram, and soon there would be a little group there. Ma would talk about the sanctity of that water, and everyone would be inspired to clear the space, remove the twigs and leaves, and help restore the proper flow of water.

As dusk fell, the mothers would walk to the kitchen area, where the ladies would be preparing vegetables for the night. They would sit with them and join in stringing beans or peeling potatoes. Often, there were far too many ladies for a small quantity of vegetables. The charm, for all of them, was the opportunity to be with Ma and to listen to her words. Light conversation would ensue and many a lesson would be imparted. Ma always emphasized on purity of thought and the importance of taking god's name while preparing food.

*

Evening arati would be at 6 p.m., and the mothers would go into their room. The rest of us would attend the evening prayers in the temples.

Later in the night, when the dinner bell rang, we would all have the evening meal in the dining hall. Ma and Chhoti Mataji would go to the Doodh Kaksha to partake of bhog prasad. Maharaj ji had once said, 'Amma, sab aahaar dooshit ho jaaygaa. Ramdana[3] hi shuddhh bachegaa. Tu aur main ramdana khaayenge.' (Amma, all food will get contaminated one day. Only ramdana will remain pure. You and I will have ramdana.)

And so, Ma would take a little bit of ramdana with milk after dinner every night.

*

After the evening prayers and before the mothers retired for the night, the elderly ladies of Kainchi would gather in the

---

[3] Amaranth.

carpet room. Chhoti Mataji and Ma would join them there. They would all share stories of Maharaj ji, of their experiences with him, and anecdotes from their pilgrimages. Sometimes there would be gentle laughter. The protocol that governed the ashram during the day faded and a feeling of joyful camaraderie took over. Youngsters such as myself would remain on the margins, but we too enjoyed the sense of freedom that crept into the room and felt ourselves a part of this very ethereal gathering.

This is when I got to hear from the old ladies that, often, when they sat with Maharaj ji, he would tell them to go inside, to Ma, saying, 'Mai[4] ke paas jaao. Ram se adhik Ram kar daasa.'

Go, sit with Mai. Greater than Ram is the servant of Ram.

---

[4] Maharaj ji would address Ma as Mai. In general, the word 'Mai'—an informal derivative of 'Ma'—was used to refer to all the elderly ladies who lived in the ashram or came for darshan.

Chapter 7

After Maharaj ji took mahasamadhi in 1973, many were disheartened, many inconsolable, and many felt lost. It was the irresistible, magnetic pull of Ma's divine love that drew thousands back to Baba Maharaj. Ma's message, 'Guru ajar amar hota hai' (Guru is immortal), reached every heart, and her constant reminder of Maharaj ji's words to all devotees, 'Tum mujhe chhor doge, main kabhi nahi chhorunga' (You may leave me but I will never leave you), began to give solace to many.

If Maharaj ji was like the wind, then Ma was like a sail that had caught the wind to steer the boat. Within a period of three years of Maharaj ji leaving his mortal form, Ma's sankalpa, her solemn resolve, led to the completion and the subsequent consecration of Maharaj ji's temple. The sun burst forth through the clouds once again; Kainchi was immersed in devotion and bliss. And with Ma's deep compassion and her peerless guru bhakti, it was as though the atmosphere in the ashram was infused with new spiritual energy.

Now that I was living in the ashram in Kainchi, every day I witnessed the never-ending streams of people who came to Ma, and the varied scenes in the darshan room remain vivid in my mind to this day.

Around 10 a.m., Ma would be seated either in the little room where I had met her for the first time, or what we called the carpet room—the galeeche wala kamra—talking to people who had come from far and wide, from all walks of life. I would slip into the crowded room quietly and sit or stand in a far corner. My first opportunity at seva came when I was called to translate the conversations Ma had with foreign visitors who had come for her darshan. But on most days, I was happy to simply bask in Ma's presence. Chhoti Mataji was always there with her. In fact, it was here that I first observed their deep bond, and how, at every moment, they would anticipate and complement each other.

Ma would welcome everyone in her warm and affectionate way, asking people about their journeys, how various family members were, often asking even after their children and grandchildren by name. Everyone was startled by how she remembered small, seemingly insignificant details about their lives. Then, Ma and Chhoti Mataji would take turns as they told a particular story about Maharaj ji's leela. Someone might sing a bhajan for them, a child might recite the Hanuman Chalisa, a Westerner might offer a hymn. A few people were so overcome by her presence that tears would flow from their eyes through the entire duration of the audience. I observed how each seeker had their own bond with Ma and, in their heart of hearts, they all felt that she was theirs, and theirs alone.

When people talked about their problems, Ma would tell them to pray to Hanuman ji, often quoting from the Ramayana: 'Kavan soh kaaj kathin jag mahi/ jo nahi hoye tat tum pahi',[1] and the Hanuman Chalisa: 'Sankat katen miten sab peera/ jo sumire Hanumat bal bira.'[2] Ma would listen attentively to each member of the gathering, giving them her affectionate guidance. One thing, however, was apparent to me and to the others present. For Ma, it was *always* Maharaj ji. To anyone who sought her blessings, she would say, 'Pray to Maharaj ji, Maharaj ji will take care of everything.'

People asked Ma to give names to the babies who had been brought to her for blessings, and many of these fortunate children were bestowed with her favourite names: Radha, Rukmini, Raghavendra, Dhananjay, Madhav. People asked Ma for little mementoes—a locket of Maharaj ji, a book, a photograph—and she would send the young girls attending to fetch these. Someone would have brought a notebook, and Ma would have the patience to inscribe 'Ram Ram' in it. I was surprised to note how the worried expressions of a few people would invariably be replaced by a sense of peace and contentment, even if they only got a fleeting moment with Ma.

Later, I sensed that if someone in the room had a specific question for Ma that they hesitated to ask in front of others, they would find that Ma had intuited it and gone on to answer

---

[1] 'Is there any task so great and difficult in this world/That you cannot accomplish, Elder Brother?' (words addressed rhetorically to Hanuman ji).

[2] 'Suffering is removed, pain is alleviated/The moment you remember the name of Hanuman.'

them, albeit in a conversation with a third person—so sensitive was she to their pride, their circumstances, or their sense of privacy. There were, also in the room, a few devotees, who had brought very humble offerings for Ma that they were reluctant to place in front of her in full view of the gathering. Ma would smile at them, and with child-like eagerness say, 'Mere liye kya laayaa? Laa de mujhe!' (What have you brought for me? Come, give it to me!) Their inhibitions would vanish in a second. And whatever it was that they had brought, Ma would partake a little of it, and share the rest with everyone.

*

One day, Ma was sitting in the darshan room. It was about 12 noon. An elderly couple requested to come in. With them was a young girl who was weeping and had to be helped into the room. After offering pranaam, they told Ma that their daughter had lost her husband within a few months of her marriage. They hoped that Ma's darshan would help in alleviating her grief. The father of the girl continued to tell Ma of the son-in-law's fatal disease and how painful it was for them to see their daughter widowed at such a young age. Then, there was complete silence in the room. The girl continued to weep. Ma looked visibly moved. But, to my surprise, she did not speak a word.

I was standing on one side, silently praying in my heart to Ma that she would say a few words to the girl to give solace in her grief. But Ma remained quiet. Soon the lunch bell rang. Ma gave prasad to the family and told me to show them the way to the dining hall in the ashram. Ma got up and went inside. I asked the family to follow me. We had barely crossed to the inner chamber of the ashram when the girl called out to her mother and said that something strange had happened to her. She said the pain of grief was no more in her heart! She was instead feeling very light, and she had not experienced such peace before. She was actually smiling. Her whole countenance had changed. Almost happy, the family proceeded for lunch.

'Gurustva mounam vyakhnam'—I realized the truth in these words. The silence of the guru is more powerful than the guru's words.

*

Another day, it was still early in the morning when a devotee arrived at the ashram and requested to see Ma urgently. Wasting no time, Ma came to the darshan room.

Ashwini told Ma that he was in acute pain for a couple of days. He had collapsed at home and had to be taken to the hospital, where he was advised immediate surgery. However, he chose to leave the hospital and came to Kainchi instead, to seek Ma's blessings. Ma heard him out and gently reprimanded him for ignoring medical advice.

Then, looking towards me, she said, 'Isko corduroy ke jhole se ek lal goli de dey aur ek takat ki goli bhi.' (Give him a red tablet and an energy tablet from my corduroy bag.) I knew that one was a mild analgesic and the other was a vitamin B capsule.

What I could make out from Ashwini's conversation with Ma was that he had some kind of an acute problem. I couldn't figure out what an ordinary painkiller or vitamin capsule would do for him. I hesitated for a second. Ma asked me again to go and get a glass of water along with the medicines.

Ma took the tablets, and after playing with them in her hands for a second or two, she gave them to Ashwini. After he had ingested the tablets, he was told to return immediately. He went home.

Ashwini did not need to return to the hospital after that. The problem did not recur.

*

Jeff Skoll, the first president of eBay and a renowned philanthropist, arrived in Kainchi one afternoon. He was accompanied by Dr Larry Brilliant, a devotee of Maharaj ji and a pioneering epidemiologist who had played a vital role in the eradication of smallpox in India. We had no prior information about their visit, nor did we have any idea of their eminence in the modern-day world.

They were invited for an audience with Ma that evening, in the galeeche wala kamra. Ma was seated on a folded black blanket—a very unostentatious setting. I was called to translate. Larry introduced Jeff to Ma. Ma was very happy as Larry recalled his memories of days with Maharaj ji in Kainchi. Ma laughed when Larry expressed his regret that he had not met Ma in the earlier days. He said he would often see Jivanti Mataji cross the ashram courtyard, who otherwise remained indoors, and only those sent by Maharaj ji were able to go to the mothers. In Larry's words, Maharaj ji did not give him a visa to Ma.

Jeff and Larry were again with Ma the next morning. Larry requested if Jeff could be allowed to visit Baba's kuti. Ma asked me to show them the way. Once inside the kuti, Larry spoke briefly, and the two men sat in silence for a while. Coming out into the courtyard behind the kuti, Larry showed Baba's chair to Jeff, briefly telling him how he met Maharaj ji here.

At that point, Ma walked in from the other side of the courtyard. She casually picked up a small stone from the pebbled courtyard and gave it to Jeff. On receiving it, Jeff was visibly moved, and Larry asked him the reason for it. Jeff then related that when he was in Afghanistan during his travels, he met a soothsayer who told him that at some point on his travels, he would be given a white stone and that would mark the apex of his journey.

Ma had given him a white stone.

*

A very distinct feature of the darshan mela was that there was an abundant flow of prasad here. As in Maharaj ji's time, Ma was very particular that every visitor to the darshan room should receive some prasad before leaving. Since the number of visitors had increased tremendously from Maharaj ji's time, Chhoti Mataji would have the prasad distributed in an organized, yet simple way.

Packets of puris, dry potato curry and cooked black gram, that had been freshly made that morning, would be brought to mother when she sat in the darshan room. The scene on the outside verandah was like a relay race; baskets would be brought in filled with prasad from the Doodh Kaksh, and empty baskets taken out to be refilled. Every one present secretly desired to receive the prasad from her hands, and before they left, Ma would gracefully hand out a packet to each one present.

If people brought fruits, Ma would distribute these then and there. The surplus would be sent to the dining hall for those who may have got left out. When devotees offered her a box of laddus or any other form of sweets as prasad, she would hold the box in her hand for a minute or so—on rare occasions take a pinch of it—and distribute the sweets to those present there or give it back to be taken home. Small packets prepared, containing sugar crystals, puffed lotus seeds and dried rose petals from flowers offered to Maharaj ji in the temple, were given as prasad to devotees from the West since they had long distances to travel. Ma used to say, 'Prasad se hriday parivartan hota hai.' (Sanctified food has the power to transmute the heart.)

Speaking of this spiritual power of prasad, a chapatti or a piece of malpua would be given by Ma as medicine for many ailments. In the room adjoining Ma's kuti, in a big wooden cupboard was stored a basket of prasad from the Jagannath Temple in Puri, sacred water from the 'Koti Teertham' in Rameshwaram, and a jar full of dried grains of rice from bhog offered at Badrinath.

I saw that, for Ma, prasad was not limited to food. It could be a flower given by Ma, a picture of Maharaj ji, the handkerchief she held in her hand and also, as we have seen in the Jeff Skoll anecdote, pebbles. Pilgrims returning from Kailash would bring stones for Ma and she would give these out to people who came that day. Whenever we went to Chitrakoot, like children, we climbed Kamadgiri Hill, collected stones and gave them to Ma. She would take them in her hand, and pointing with her finger, she would show us 'Ram' or 'Om' inscribed on them. Often, she would show the face of Hanuman ji with a mace. Ma would give out these stones as prasad, telling us that Lord Ram had lived on the Kamadgiri mountain for twelve years, and these pebbles were not stones, they were gems. Chitrakutam Manikutam.[3]

En route to Badrinath, Ma would ask for the car to be stopped near the Garur Ganga. We would sprinkle a little water upon us from the sacred river and collect stones from the riverbed. Ma would give these to people who frequently came across snakes in their houses. She would ask them to keep these stones in the house and the snakes would not be seen after that.

---

[3]   The stones of Chitrakut are gems.

Chapter 8

For me, in the ashram in Kainchi, Maharaj ji's kuti is the sanctum sanctorum. Over the years, it had been kept by Ma and Chhoti Mataji just as it had been in his lifetime—it was almost as though one could feel his divine presence here. It was in this sacred place, that Maharaj ji, the eternal guru, had bade his goodbye to Ma, the eternal disciple, with the deeply moving words: 'Teen kaal mein kahu ne na aisi seva kari, na kou karega. Sansaar ko haste hue chhodunga, tujh ko rote hue chhodunga.' (In three ages, no one has served the way you have, and no one ever will. I will leave the world laughing, but I will weep leaving you.) This had signalled the transition from Maharaj to Ma.

One of the changes in the room though, Ma told me, were the photographs of Baba. Before she did arati in the kuti as a part of her morning puja, Chhoti Ma would wipe these clean with Ganga water. She would handpick flowers herself, and during puja, place these in a beautiful way in front of Baba's photographs. The other addition to the room was a glass-covered shelf, in which Ma kept treasured relics such as his

Ma offering incense by Maharaj ji's chair in Kainchi

Ram Ram notebooks, his clothes, his thali, his fire tongs and his last train ticket to Vrindavan. Also safeguarded by the mothers was the pitcher filled with clay that Baba used to wash his hands with.[1]

Food cooked in the ashram kitchen was brought in a thali, just as it was done in Maharaj ji's time. Ma would offer the

---

[1] In those days, soap used animal fat in addition to chemicals, and so Maharaj ji used only clay to wash his hands.

bhog, and then the plate was taken back to the kitchen, the prasad mixed in all the food that had been cooked.

The kuti opened into a small pebbled courtyard, where Maharaj ji often used to sit in the sun, on a wooden chair. During a few occasions, it served as a small meeting place. Sometimes, Ma and Chhoti Mataji would help him bathe there.

One day, a devotee came to Maharaj ji and offered to have the place cemented, since he felt that the pebbles must be hurting Baba's feet. Maharaj ji agreed. Ma had overheard the conversation. Finding a quiet moment, she began to collect the pebbles in the pallu of her dhoti. When Maharaj ji asked her what she was doing, Ma said the pebbles were precious as they bore the touch of his feet. She was collecting them now, as they would probably be thrown away when the cementing was done.

That very moment, Maharaj ji sent a message to the devotee that the backyard would remain as it was.

The same pebbles are there even today. When the walls are being painted or repairs are being carried out in Maharaj ji's kuti, the stones are picked up carefully and stored. Later, they are washed and replaced in Maharaj ji's courtyard. Here too, Ma would spontaneously pick up a stone and point out, to whoever was present, the letters R-A-M (in Devanagari script) on it, later giving the stones away as prasad. Maharaj ji often said to her, 'Amma teri aakhon me ram nam hai.' (Ma you have Ram-naam in your eyes.)

*

Two days before Maharaj ji's final departure from Kainchi, he had asked Ma and Chhoti Mataji to start living in the kuti adjacent to his. This is where they lived now. Gradually Ma started meeting me here. As entry into the mothers' room was limited to very few, I took this as a sign of my acceptance.

That was when I observed how Ma's room was as simple as Baba's kuti. There were two wooden beds on either side of the room, covered with coarse woollen blankets, both black in colour. On Ma's side of the room, books and photographs of Maharaj ji were kept on the window ledge. Next to Chhoti Ma's bed were a few racks built into the wall. On that, along with photographs of Maharaj ji, was a framed photo of Hanuman ji, which I recognized was a picture postcard I had sent to Ma during one of my journeys to Rameshwaram. Next to it was a small rock, which I had picked up, and sent to Ma from the Kamadgiri mountain in Chitrakoot. On the topmost shelf, an iron spatula was kept. The first time I noticed it, I observed it had been worshipped with flowers and sandalwood paste.

Ma told me that the paltaa had been given to her by a sadhu, who had blessed her with the words, 'Teraa chhakachhak bhandara chalegaa, kabhi kamee nahin hogee.' (You will have plenty to feed people with, there will never be a shortage of sacred food.) From then on, for every bhandara, the spatula is ceremoniously taken on a steel plate to the cooking venue, preceded by the sound of conch shells and the ringing of bells and the sprinkling of Ganga water. The cooking is started with this spatula and then it is placed in the kitchen altar. It is brought back at night to Ma's room, only after everyone has been fed.

This simple room was devoid of any personal possessions. All that the mothers had were two sets of clothes, a beige sweater and a beige hill-woven shawl each, neatly kept in two cane baskets. These were kept in the wooden cupboard in the Doodh Kaksh. The mothers always wore white khadi dhotis. Devotees would offer them new dhotis and they would, of course, accept them with the love with which these had been brought. But later, Ma would distribute the new dhotis to sadhus, or give them away to the Mai-s. In fact, Ma would give away *whatever* came to her. She would often say, 'Sanchay karna achha nahi . . . Ishwar kabhi koi kami nahi karta.' (It is not good to accumulate . . . God never keeps us in dearth.)

Another very special article that I associate with the mothers was a small cloth bag made of beige corduroy fabric, and it travelled with Ma whenever she went on a journey. Ma was never seen to carry it herself though; someone accompanying her would remember to take it for her. We all fondly called it the 'corduroy ka jhola'!

This bag had almost everything that might be needed by Maharaj ji in the years that the mothers travelled with him: a small penknife to peel fruit for him, a small pouch of roasted gram-flour seasoned with carom seeds and salt in case Maharaj ji's meals were delayed, some simple ayurvedic medicines like Amritdhara, 'kanthi' for the throat, and some carminative salts. In the bag were also a few tablets of Anacin and capsules of Becosule, and the most amazing cures were performed with these two. Also in the bag was a candle and a box of matches. There were no generators on railway platforms in those days, and it was a common phenomenon that the supply of electricity would be cut off every now and then, making it very inconvenient for Maharaj ji to board the train. On many occasions, then and later, Ma's candle in the corduroy bag would come in handy.

*

The most precious moment for me in Kainchi came one winter evening. Ma called me to her kuti and said that from now on I was to stay with the mothers in their room. I couldn't believe it!

This signalled a moment of great transition in my life, as I became a part of their inner world.

In the evening, Ma sat on her takhat and wrote Ram Ram in her notebook. Chhoti mataji sat on her takhat, eyes closed and meditative. Ma told me to read out the Srimad Devi Bhagvat to them. It became a routine with me to sit on a folded blanket upon the wooden floor and read out the sacred text to the mothers.

My joy at being given this opportunity to read to the mothers daily was slightly marred by my lack of fluency in reading the Hindi text. So, in the mornings, I put myself to task and prepared for the evenings, reading the text chapter by chapter, line by line, several times. Even then, it remained a struggle.

One day, as I was crossing the temple area, I heard Sanskrit shlokas from the Bhagavad Gita being chanted near Baba's temple. I was drawn in by the perfect enunciation and went in to see who it was.

It turned out to be a young girl I knew, Shakuntala, who was physically disabled. She was reading the Sanskrit shlokas of the Bhagavad Gita out loud. I was amazed at this because Shakuntala had never received any formal education or schooling in her life. When I asked her the secret of her eloquence, she told me that Maharaj ji had once placed his hand on her head and blessed her, saying 'Tu to Vyaas hai' or 'You, my child, are Vyaas.'[2] Since that day, she was able to read the most difficult of texts with great felicity. Totally taken in with this story, my whole day went in silent prayers to Maharaj ji for a similar boon, —all in the pursuit of perfection so my evening readings to Ma would be faultless.

The next morning, a scantily clad sadhu appeared at Maharaj ji's temple. He wore a muddy cloth wrapped around his waist and a thin blanket over his shoulders. I saw both mothers proceed towards him from Ma's kuti, and I followed. A brief conversation ensued between them. The sadhu said that he had just walked all the way from Badrinath. The distance from Badrinath to Kainchi was over 300 kilometres. The mothers requested him to stay a day and rest in the ashram.

He replied, 'Sant sukhi vicharant mahi.' (A sadhu is happy wandering.)

And then, just before he turned to go, he said to me, 'Aur tum, tum to Vyaas ho.'

And you, you are Vyaas.

---

[2] Traditionally, the learned sage who was elucidating on the scriptures at any given time was given the honorific of 'Vyaas' after the great Krishna Dwaipayan Vyasa, who is believed to be the compiler of the Mahabharata and the classifier of the Vedas.

Chapter 9

Ma emphasized that bhakti[1] without seva[2] and seva without bhakti were meaningless. She would remind everyone that Maharaj ji used to say, 'Guru ke adrishya hone par Guru sthaan hi Guru swaroop ho jata hai.' (When the Guru leaves his mortal frame, his place—his ashram— assumes the significance of his form.) In time, the ashram in Kainchi came to reflect this. With the exception of a few employees, the entire place was managed collectively by devotees, who came whenever they could, and performed their allotted tasks with great love.

One of things that distinguished the Kainchi ashram was the impeccable cleanliness of the premises. This is something Ma was very particular about. As she walked around, nothing escaped her eye. Any place that needed washing, cleaning, dusting or polishing would be on the agenda for the next day. The temples, of course, were spotless, and the poshaak[3]

---

[1] Devotion.
[2] Selfless service.
[3] Ceremonial raiments.

of the deities through the seasons were kept in an extremely organized manner. The puja lamps, the trays and bells were so well-polished that visitors often mistook the brass for gold. The mothers ensured that even small details were not neglected. For instance, the blankets from the rooms were put out in the sun periodically; the quilt covers and bedsheets duly washed. Ma's eye did not miss even the dog's bowl. If it hadn't been cleaned properly, she would immediately send for the man responsible for this.

The other thing which set Kainchi apart was that wastage of any kind was intolerable to Ma. I remember an incident from when I was still a newcomer in the ashram. One morning, I was alone in the back veranda with Ma. The pujari came and left a jute sack full of sweet lime with us, saying that someone had brought these. Ma asked me to get a pair of scissors and open it. She told me to place the fruit in a wide round basket in such a way that there was no overlapping or bruising of the limes. After I did this, she sent me to give the hay in the bag to the night watchman, to be used in the fire for the water heater the next morning. Then the gunny bag was given to the kitchen, to be used as a mop for scrubbing the floor. It did not end here. The twine with which the bag had been stitched was neatly rolled up and kept in a cardboard box. This would be used later, to tie up the folded mats and rugs when the ashram closed for the winter. This was perhaps my greatest practical lesson in putting everything to effective use. *Nothing* was to be wasted.

After this, Ma reminded me of the photograph of Maharaj ji, kept in Ma's kuti, which shows a tear in Maharaj ji's eye. She told me that this was when Maharaj ji had found some rotis that had been thrown away in the ashram, and it had caused him immense pain. Ma quoted him on this, 'Ashram mein daan ka paisa hai. Log apna kharcha kam karke yahaan daan dete hain. Kabhi koi cheez barbaad mat karo.' (The money in the ashram has been donated by people. They sacrifice their own needs and give the money here. Never waste anything.)

Over the years, I heard Ma repeat these words time and again.

*

The high level of maintenance and cleanliness in Kainchi was carried out by the Mai-s. Living in the ashram and devoting themselves wholly to Maharaj ji's seva were a group of elderly ladies, some of whom had been widowed, some of whom lived in the ashram with their husbands, and all of them deeply devoted to Ma. Dressed austerely in their preferred white dhotis, and spending the whole day attending to the needs of the ashram, they were the elderly gopis[4] of Kainchi. So dedicated were they to Ma that they would carry out her wishes even before she had articulated them.

Speaking of the Mai-s, a story comes to mind. During the consecration of Maharaj ji's temple, when the ashram was full of visitors, the electricity transformer blew out one night.

---

[4] The cowherd maidens of Vrindavan, renowned for their great love for Sri Krishna.

Ma and Jivanti ma with the Mai-s in Kainchi

Kainchi was engulfed in darkness, and Ma and Chhoti Mataji seemed disturbed. I was told that the Mai-s, undeterred by this setback, procured large quantities of ghee from the store and lit a thousand or more deeyas in the ashram. When she saw the beauty of this impromptu Diwali that had descended upon Kainchi on this holy day, Ma had smiled and told the Mai-s that they had brought Maharaj ji's prophecy to fruition. Many years ago, he had said, 'Mai, dekhnaa, ek din yahan ghee ke deeye jalenge.' (Mai, you will see, one day lamps with ghee will be lit in Kainchi.)

Even though I came from a very different world—not that I ever saw it in those terms—the Mai-s enveloped me in their warm affections, caring for me as their own. Sometimes I would find that my torn socks had been silently darned and placed on my bed. If I ever missed a meal, one of them would seek me out and reprimand me for not eating properly. When I fell sick, the Mai-s would prepare convalescent food, and I still remember the taste of the 'jaula' they would make. However, it wasn't just me. No one who came to Kainchi could miss the care and bounteous love of the Mai-s.

*

As I gained deeper insights into Ma's inner world, I got to know a few people, who were conspicuous of their proximity to Ma, despite their non-conformist ways. It seemed they were not bound by the ashram etiquette and were free to see Ma whenever they chose to visit her. I was initially unable to understand this, but later I was moved by Ma's affinity to them.

I remember Panuli didi, an old woman who lived in the ashram, in a small kuti below my room. In time, I came to feel that she was a little watch guard for me, shouting out at the slightest noise in the vicinity. Looking out from my window, past midnight, I would often see her walking around the inner courtyard, talking loudly, as if in communion with someone else. Diminutive and dark, Panuli Didi wore a long cotton skirt with a sweater and a warm shawl. On her eyes were a pair of old black spectacles, that was tied at the back with a string. Her matted hair was rarely combed.

Not much is known about her origins or where she came from, and perhaps she never had any family of her own, because all the years she lived in Kainchi, we saw no one visit her. Panuli didi spent her time picking husk and stones from grains used in the ashram kitchen. She would also clean the garden.

Such were her ways that sometimes the staff in Kainchi would lose their patience with her. Never Ma. She might have strange moods and fancies, but Ma would bear them all with loving kindness. Almost every day, when Ma went around the ashram, she would make it a point to walk by her and share a few words with her.

Sometimes Panuli didi would be sitting near Maharaj ji's rock, clapping her hands and singing 'Maharaj ji halu banao, halu banao!' Ma would then order halwa to be made in the kitchen that day. Often, before leaving for a journey, whether to Vrindavan or Rishikesh, Ma would gently tease her. 'Come with me, Panuli didi. I will show you Vrindavan.' That day she would hide herself and wouldn't be found the whole day. Panuli didi never left Kainchi.

In her last few days, she fell very sick. Ma asked the Mai-s in the ashram to do the Hanuman Chalisa paath in her kuti. One morning, Ma sent a message that the chanting of Hanuman Chalisa should be stopped, and the Gajendra Moksha should be read. Instead of water, she should be given teaspoons of Gangajal. That very evening Panuli passed away.

Another favourite with Maharaj ji and Ma was Lohni ji, who had been given the name 'Babu Sahab' or 'Respected Sir' by Maharaj ji. At any spiritual event, such as the chanting of the

Ramayana or the recitation of Srimad Bhagvat, or any temple bhandara, Babu Sahab was sure to be seen. Dressed in a khadi kurta and pyjama and a Gandhi cap, rarely clean, he could walk up to Maharaj ji whenever he chose to. He never asked for anything, but Maharaj ji would tell the devotees sitting around him to give him money for his bus fare to Nainital. This continued in Ma's time also.

Often the young boys in the ashram would tease him, and Babu Sahab, in tears, would rush to Ma, wherever she was. He used to address her as 'Siddhi Didi'. Ma might have been sitting with high-ranking officials and judges at the time, but she would instantly set everyone aside to listen to Babu Sahab's tale of woe. Someone would have called him 'baagad billu' or wildcat; someone else might have sprayed some water on him from the hosepipe in the garden. The offending boy would be called immediately, and Ma would patiently explain to him that the childlike Babu Sahab was a very good soul, and we would incur sin on ourselves if we made him unhappy. The matter would be settled and Babu Sahab would leave Kainchi satisfied, with money for his bus ticket. Years later, when his time was close, Ma sent him to Vrindavan on a bus, and it was in the ashram in Vrindavan that he breathed his last.

One was a Nepalese man called Moti. Today, at about sixty years of age, I was told that he had found his way to Kainchi as a small boy, walking the whole distance from his hometown in Nepal. He lived in the village alone in a small shack, earning his livelihood by working as a farmhand or by grazing cows. He was never seen to associate with any of the

village folk, choosing to spend his life in an orbit around Ma—
in a very silent way—and as far as I know, he never travelled
out of Kainchi.

Moti would climb the hills overlooking the ashram with
the cows, getting Ma's darshan from there. Occasionally, he
would come to meet Ma and directly walk into the inner rooms
of the ashram. Ma would welcome him as one of her very own.
She would have a bag of namkeen or peanuts or even roasted
gram saved up for him. Every winter, Ma remembered to keep
aside two sets of woollen clothing, a quilt and a warm blanket
for Moti. These were given to him by Ma herself as he would
not accept it from anyone else.

Moti continues to live in the village and every now and
then, I meet him outside the ashram. I will never forget that
when Ma's last rites were being performed at the ghat in
Haridwar, in that huge crowd I had seen Moti next to me, his
hair dishevelled, his clothes in disarray. He stood in silence, his
face wet with tears.

Today as I write these words, I am transported to Kainchi
of that time, and I can perhaps see even more clearly than I
could then, how Ma had a place in her heart for those people
who were disregarded by society, and who had no place in the
world. Not loved by anyone, they were loved by her.

Chapter 10

The most important event of Kainchi was, and continues to be, the bhandara held on 15 June every year.

Way before dawn, the scene begins to unfold. The temples in the ashram, always so serene and calm, today reverberate with spiritual energy. Golden streamers, coloured ribbons and decorative flags adorn all of Kainchi. The deities are dressed in their new poshaak, the gold borders of their garments adding to the grandeur. The prayers of so many have invoked their divinity that the murtis in each temple seem to manifest a heightened magical aura, so sublime, so alive, altogether above this world. The courtyard bustles with activity as the sevaks run around to give final touches to their tasks. Many would not have slept the night before, yet there is no sign of fatigue in their movements. Joy is writ large on every face. 'Aaj pandrah June hai!' (Today is 15 June!)

As the sun rises, the entire range of surrounding hills is transformed into a riot of colours. Packed buses and cars ply back and forth. Streams of people, some having walked miles on the rocky terrain, descend the hills into the valley of Kainchi. Women wearing their new sarees saved for the day; men from the villages in well-washed clothes; children in festive apparel with bold dots of collyrium on their foreheads so as to not attract the evil eye. The crowds begin to gather on the road, waiting with great patience for an early entry into the temples to get darshan, and thereafter, to receive the sacred malpua prasad, for which many have waited all year through.

Meanwhile, inside the ashram, it is time for the bhog prasad to be carried to the temples. The blowing of conches, the beating of the nagaaras, and the sound of gongs and bells herald the bhandara open. Thalis of Malpua prasad, covered with crimson velvet thaal-poshes, is ceremoniously carried by a group of men in a procession to the temples, preceded by the

15 June celebration in Ma's divine presence

sprinkling of Ganga water. The devotees in the ashram follow them, and the air is filled with calls of Neem Karoli Baba ki Jai, Mataji ki Jai, Chhoti Maiyya ki Jai. The ladies gather and shower flower petals as the bhog passes by. After being offered at the temples, the malpuas are brought back to the cooking venue and mixed with the rest.

Now the gates are opened. And within moments, the ashram is full of people. The feeding starts.

*

It is intriguing that the specific date of 15 June was chosen by Maharaj ji for the consecration of all the temples in Kainchi from the Gregorian calendar, rather than selecting a traditional auspicious tithi from the Hindu almanac. One of the reasons for this could be that the tithi varies from year to year, whereas a set date from the calendar would be convenient for all to remember. The other reason could be that Maharaj ji chose the month of June so that the devotees coming from far away could get a brief respite from the blistering heat of the plains in summer and stay in the cool mountain air for a few days.

In the year 1976, Ma too chose the date of 15 June for the prana pratishtha[1] of Maharaj ji's murti in his temple. That year, the month of June, according to the astrological chart, fell in the Purshottam Maas, in which no auspicious ceremonies

---

[1] A symbolic ritual whereby life is invoked in an idol, by a priest, as he chants mantras.

are performed. The acharyas and scholars requested Ma to reconsider the day, but she would have none of it. Ma was adamant that if Maharaj ji chose the date of 15 June for the temples, it had to be the same for Maharaj ji's mandir as well.

Perhaps the most significant aspect, which spiritually energized the bhandara, was Ma's strong emphasis on the power of the god's name. The maha mantra kirtan singers from Vrindavan would start their chanting at the Vaishnavi Devi Temple near the main gate in mid-April, which would go on till the end of Navratri in October. A month before the bhandara, the akhand Hanuman Chalisa paath[2] would begin in Maharaj ji's temple. Devotees would take turns to recite the Chalisa day and night, concluding on the morning of 14 June. As the date for the bhandara drew closer, the Mai-s would circumambulate the boundary of the ashram, singing the Hanuman Chalisa—after which they would sit in different spots, be it the kitchen, at the main gates, by the two bridges, in the yagyashala,[3] wherever, to do their personal sadhana. In this way, every inch of the sacred bhoomi of Kainchi was redolent with the purest vibrations.

For many years, the Srimad Bhagvat saptah, the week-long reading of the Bhagwat Purana was done in a very festive way in the yagyashala, also concluding a day before the bhandara. Later, the rendering of the *Ramcharitmanas* by sadhus from Vrindavan was organized for nine days. Their colloquial style

---

[2] Uninterrupted recitation of Hanuman Chalisa.

[3] The sacred place where fire oblations are made to propitiate deities for the welfare of the world.

of singing, in which the rhythm varied in accordance with the themes of the text, left each one enraptured. The completion of the reading of the Ramayana culminated with the bhandara.

While these recitations were on during the daytime, the evenings would have a special soft ending. The Mai-s, done with their seva, would gather in the yagyashala and sing bhajans. The rhythmic beat of the dholak, accompanied by the cymbals, would add to the festive hue. Few of the aged Mai-s, at times seventy and above, would spontaneously get up and dance to a devi bhajan. Their eyes closed, their faces reflecting the bliss they were immersed in. Sometimes, Ma could be observed standing by the window of the darshan room, watching them from afar, amused by their sprightliness.

As is evident by now, June was an exceptionally busy month. All the activities were shared by the volunteers who came from near and far, from different communities and classes, but all mingled together inside the ashram, united by the one thing common to them all—their intense desire to serve. Ma's constant reminders to the seekers over the years, 'Maharaj ji se prarthna karo . . . Maharaj ji sab sunte hain . . . Maharaj ji sab karenge . . . Guru devon ka dev' (Pray to Maharaj ji . . . Maharaj ji listens to everything . . . Maharaj ji will do everything . . . The Guru is the god of the gods), began to echo in every heart, and the devotees, old and new, began to see Maharaj ji through Ma. Just one glimpse, one word from her, would send forth a new wave of devotional fervour among them. Consequently, the bhandara which started with a few hundreds, now swelled to include hundreds of thousands.

On the morning of 1 June, Arjan Das ji arrived with his group, all the way from Chennai. A prosperous businessman, known widely for his philanthropic activities, Arjan Dada was the true backbone of the bhandara. Readily internalizing Ma's instructions, Dada, with his remarkable organizational skills, would oversee every aspect of the preparations from that day on. Ma would say, 'Ab Dada aa gaye. Pandrah June shuru ho gaya!' (Now that Dada has come, 15 June has begun!)

Now onwards, it was an incredible scene: people pouring in every day to volunteer their services in the bhandara. After the initial audience with Ma, they would merge in the sea of seva, eager to do their utmost. Most of the men would proceed to the malpua section, ready to take up the challenging tasks there. Fighting sleep, ignoring fatigue, they would be lost to the world for the next few days. The seniors would participate in organizational work; the youngsters in more strenuous activities. The ladies would take over the management of the daily kitchen, ensuring the pristine cleanliness of the ashram. As early as 2 a.m., the girls would be seen mopping the floors, activities would commence in the kitchen to prepare the day's meals, and the pujaris would be rushing to bathe. The elders were already engrossed in their sadhana. All of them yearned for the moment when Ma would come by on her morning round.

In the initial years with Maharaj ji, the bhandara was a day-long event. The cooking of malpua and aloo sabzi—the set menu which continues to this day—would start in the morning, and, by evening, everything would be cleared up. By the 1980s Ma's divine aura had spread far and wide. As a result, the bhandara began to assume a mammoth form and the number of people coming to Kainchi went up exponentially. To provide prasad for the thousands that came, the number of cooks had to be increased each year, and the cooking had to be done round the clock, eventually starting five days in advance.

The traditional way of preparing the prasad is still maintained. The malpuas are cooked in huge iron woks, in large fire-pits. These fire stoves are made by digging pits in the earth, and wood is used for fuel. The making of malpuas is a culinary skill which is passed from generation to generation in the villages of western Uttar Pradesh. The cooks are hired from here. These men, simple at heart but highly accomplished in their work, take turns to cook in the intense heat of the bhattis. Occasionally, one got to see streaks of zealous fervour in these men. The leader of the cooks was Shanti, a thin, dark man, possessing unusual energy. Once, a passer-by happened to ask him how they managed to work in the fumes and the heat. Shanti looked up from the wok in front of him, in which the ghee was boiling. Without a word, he dipped both his hands into the ghee.

As is the observance, prasad is never tasted before it is offered as bhog. And so, determining the quality of the prasad and whether the malpua had been cooked properly or not, was dependent on Ma's amazing perception. Samples of malpuas from every fresh stock were carried to her on the hour. Ma would take one out of the basket and in her hand, turn it over, feeling the thickness. Observing closely, she would sometimes point out that the flame in the stoves should be decreased as the malpuas were being cooked on too strong a flame and so, while the outer crust was cooked, the dough inside was still undone. Ma would point out if the quantity of aniseed was not enough or if there should be less pepper. She continuously sent instructions to the cooks, even to the extent of regulating the size of the malpuas.

The cooking area was very warm and humid, and so care had to be taken that the malpuas were cooked to the right degree, and that they were properly cooled before being stored, or else there was a risk of fungus forming on them. I remember, on one occasion, a panicked message was brought to Ma that there was anxiety in the kitchen that signs of fungus were suddenly visible on the stored malpuas, even though their golden-brown colour showed that they had been properly cooked. There had been no negligence whatsoever in cooling them before they were stacked. Speculations started. Some suggested exhaust fans, others wanted air conditioners to be installed. Meanwhile, pedestal fans were placed there to help in the better flow of air.

Ma asked for the malpuas to be brought to her. After taking a look at them, she sent a young man to look around in the cooking area for something unusual. He found a few bags of brown colouring, which were being added to the dough to give the malpua the right colour, without the need of frying them for the necessary time. Hence, the malpuas were not being cooked through, and fungus was forming on them. Ma asked the bags to be removed from the kitchen, and the issue was resolved.

Unseen to the world, on the night of 14 June, the lights in Ma's kuti and in the adjoining rooms would not be turned off. Ma, with Jivanti Mataji by her side, would walk up several times to the malpua bhandar. A gentle word for each one, calling to them by their names, asking the tired to take some rest, was enough to satiate everyone. Seeing the mothers, everyone would rush to herd around them.

Back in their kuti, the mothers personally oversaw that baskets of mangoes were sent to the workers all night long. Sometimes it was de-stoned lychees or buckets of freshly made buttermilk to soothe parched throats. Bottles of Rooh-afza sharbat sent by Ma were another great favourite.

The crowd of people attending the bhandara would peak on the fourteenth. There were arrivals through the night. By then, all possible accommodation provided by the ashram would be full, leaving only the option of sleeping in the open verandahs. Ma ensured that a stock of blankets was kept aside and, past midnight, these were sent out for those who were asleep in the open. Amidst that huge crowd at night, Ma was even sensitive to the cries of babies. She would send the Mai-s to refill their feeding bottles with fresh milk, and, if necessary, provide warm wraps to them, using the extra shawls that were kept as a part of the winter poshaak of the deities in the temples. Home-remedies such as tulsi chai, aniseed decoction, kanthi for the throat, amrit dhara for stomach ailments, were kept at hand. Many times, the medicine available did not tally with the complaint, yet it was effective in giving miraculous relief.

*

We had all come to see that Ma preferred to keep away from the public at large, choosing to always stay in Maharaj ji's shadow. She only made an exception to this on 15 June, when she sat continuously, for almost ten hours in the small enclosure that had been made for her, on the front side of the terrace where the bhandara was held. Every person who had come to partake of prasad would have the privilege of Ma's darshan when they went past her. And as they offered pranaam, Ma too would fold her hands to greet them. If the elders of the ashram suggested that maybe Ma should go inside and rest for a little while, she would reply, 'Sab Maharaj ke liye aaye hain. Main sab ke darshan karoongi.' (Everyone has come for Maharaj. I would like everyone's darshan.)

From where Ma was seated, she had a full view of the feeding area, of the people in the queue walking up to the ashram, as well as of the winding road across the river. Even as she would be speaking a word or two to the constant stream of devotees, Ma would be silently assessing the crowds and sending repeated instructions to Arjan Dada—to increase the output or slow down—as the situation demanded. Sometimes, a few of Ma's instructions baffled everyone. For instance, even if we could all see that the crowds were thinning, Ma might send specific instructions to the workers to increase the output of malpuas as, she would say, there would be a huge surge after a particular time. This would invariably come true.

Except for a few sips of water, both mothers would not eat or drink anything the whole day. When the bhandara came to a close, they would return to the kuti, and the Mai-s would have tea ready for them. It was only when the last few had eaten at night that the mothers would partake a little of the malpua prasad. By now, Ma and Chhoti Mataji both looked very tired, as though completely depleted, having given of themselves so generously through the day. Barely speaking a word between them, they would retire to the kuti to rest for a few hours.

In the biography of Sri Sarada Devi, the author tells us that Ma Sarada's feet were very sensitive to the touch of some, and she would immediately get blisters in her feet with a terrible burning sensation. It was the same with Ma. Having met nearly a lakh of people that day, all eager to touch her feet and offer pranaam, by the end of the day Ma's feet would be hot like burning coals, with dark brown spots on them. We would keep jugs filled with Ganga water ready, and the moment she entered the veranda at the back, her feet were washed with it. This was known to give immediate relief. The old ladies in the ashram would whip ghee a hundred and eight times in a 'phool ki thali' (a plate made from an alloy of bronze) and apply it on Ma's feet before she slept.

The next day would begin very early for Ma. By then, the ashram looked bathed—so clean that no one could tell that thousands of people had been in Kainchi the day before. Ma would personally meet all the people who had immersed themselves in the seva, be it the devotees, the workers, the volunteers, or the families of the staff. With incredible patience she gave time to everyone, blessing them individually, and ensuring that malpuas and other prasad were packed and sent home for them. The fond leave-taking, in fact, went on for two or three days.

According the highest eminence to the event of 15 June, Ma would tell everyone, 'Yeh bhandara Maharaj ji ka viraat swaroop hai.' (This bhandara is the cosmic form of Maharaj ji.)

Even today, the 15 June bhandara is held in Kainchi with the same spirit, the same fervour.

Part II

Chapter 11

Ma and Jivanti mataji stayed in Kainchi ashram for most of the year. The ashram would be closed during the winter months, with only the essential temple services continuing. The formal reopening of the ashram was on the 16 April. It began with the singing of Ram-naam kirtan by singers from Vrindavan and this would continue for the next six months. The daily bhandara would also start from this day. Both the mothers would be in Kainchi now onwards.

The mothers would follow a certain pattern of travel during the year. After the 15 June bhandara, they would go for a retreat in the interior of the hills for a month or more. This was called the ekaantvaas, and the destination would be known only to a few. Utmost secrecy was maintained in selecting an appropriate place for their stay so that the mothers could spend an undisturbed and restful period. On their return from ekaantvaas, it would be time for Guru Purnima and Ma would go to Kainchi or proceed to Rishikesh. For Maharaj ji's punya tithi in September, Ma would invariably be in Vrindavan. Her longest continuous stay in Kainchi would be in the months of May and June and also in October for the Shardiya Navratri Pooja.

In the winter months, after the ashram closed, the mothers would often go to snow-laden Badrinath for Deepavali. After that, accompanied by a few devotees, they would begin their travels. Usually, they went southward first, to Rameshwaram or Tirupati, where the climate was warmer. From there, they might journey eastward to Jagannath Puri or westward to Dwarka. For Makar Sankranti, Ma and Chhoti Mataji were often in Prayaag, and Holi was, of course, always in Brij Bhoomi, Vrindavan. After Holi, the mothers would return to Kainchi in time for 16 April. Besides these travels, Ma would also visit Maharaj ji's temples, ashrams, and the village of Neem Karoli regularly.

*

I had often heard about Ma's travels and pilgrimages with Maharaj ji, and since then, I had begun to secretly nourish a desire to travel with Ma someday. I felt that in a different environment, without the ashram protocol and decorum, I would get to see a different side of Ma. This proximity would also help me overcome the many hesitations—the many self-imposed restraints that were in my mind.

One winter morning, on her morning round of the ashram in Kainchi, Ma walked into my room. It was unusual, so I was surprised. She sat on my bed and said, 'Chal, Poornagiri chalegi hamare saath?' (Come, will you come to Poornagiri with me?) Before I could barely stammer a reply, Ma said that we would be leaving the next morning, there would be two cars, and one of the cars would be mine.

In those days, I had a Fiat, bright apple-green in colour. That day, hoping against all hope that Ma might travel a part of the distance with me, I scrubbed the car to its soul!

As written in the Puranas, after desecrating the yajna of Prajapati Daksha, when Bhagwan Shiv was bearing aloft the body of Goddess Sati, parts of her mortal remains fell in various places, which are now known as shakti peethas. Situated at an altitude of 5500 ft on the Annapoorna range, the Poornagiri siddha peeth is in the Champavat district of Uttarakhand. It is believed that the navel of the Devi fell here. In those days, an arduous trek of about 20 kilometres through dense forests, up the rubble track up the mountain, led to the shrine.

We departed from Kainchi the next day.

The mothers commenced the journey in the Ambassador car, accompanied by the men, and the ladies in the group got into my car. After driving for two or three hours, a stop was made. The group went to a tea shop nearby. Both mothers silently disembarked from the Ambassador and came and sat in my car. From there on, Ma continued to travel in the Fiat till we returned to Kainchi. This was the start of many a drive over the next thirty-seven years in my travels with Ma.

Our base camp for the night was a forest dak bungalow at Boom, near the town of Tanakpur, on the bank of the Sharada river. After the initial cleaning of Ma's room, and a short break for rest, both mothers walked down to the riverside. The mothers sat on the rocks, and we sat near them, on the sand. I remember how appreciative Ma was of the natural beauty all around. The calm river, the long shadows of the trees, and the reddish glow of the sun. Seeing my camera slung on my shoulder—with a gentle pat upon my back—Ma asked me to feel free to take photographs. Again, this marked the beginning of my taking hundreds of photographs of the mothers and our pilgrimages over the years.

After dusk, we lit a wood fire, around which we sat and sang the evening prayers. Then we all talked for a while. Ma told us that she had been to Poornagiri Temple many years ago. I too had visited the shrine several times as a child, and we shared memories. A member of our group described to Ma a strange dream he had had the night before. He said he had seen Baba Maharaj lying down, covered with rags, asking him for a cigarette. When he offered a cigarette in the dream, Maharaj ji took two drags and handed the cigarette back to him. The dream ended there. Ma listened very attentively, though she did not say anything.

The next morning, we started early and soon we were climbing up the hill. The path was rocky and uneven. We had barely covered a short distance when Chhoti Mataji misplaced a step and fell down. Luckily, there were others around her to give immediate support. Except for a little stiffness, there was no injury as such. However, it meant that she would have to walk slowly, with help.

Ma was a habitual fast walker, and as she went ahead, I accompanied her. Making intermittent stops on the way to rest, we went past the most beautiful rivulets and waterfalls. The few pilgrims crossing our path would greet Ma with calls of 'Poornagiri Maiyya ki Jai, Parvaton vali ki Jai!'[1] Ma and I would also respond to their calls with joy. Slowly we reached a dense forest of sal trees. Though it was winter, the entire landscape was covered with auburn leaves as in autumn.

In the forest, we saw from a distance, a man lying under a tree. Wrapped in a length of tattered tarp, he had almost blended into the floor of the forest. As we neared him, he roused himself and asked a person who was passing by for a cigarette. When given one, he took two drags of it and gave it back. Someone called out to say to us there was a mad man under a tree, and that we should be careful. Ma shook her head and whispered, 'Yeh pagal nahi hain.' (He is not mad.)

As we drew close, we saw the figure lying still again, amidst the heaps of twigs and leaves. Quietly, Ma sat down beside him. I stood by, in silence. She kept looking up at the sky. Slowly, the figure moved and sat up, facing Ma. He had no clothing on his body and had covered himself with the rag. Ma spoke to him in a very soft voice, and he seemed to be answering her. Their conversation lasted a minute or two.

I had with me two apples for Ma. Taking these from me, Ma placed them gently in front of him. I was also carrying

---

[1] Glory to the Goddess of Poornagiri, glory to the one who resides in the mountains!

with me some singals, a doughnut-like preparation made in the Kumaon. Ma took a handful of these and placed them on a leaf nearby. After a moment, she picked one or two and giving them to me, said, 'Yeh yahan ka prasad hai. Isko yaheen khaa le.' (This is prasad from this place. Eat it here right now.)

The man covered himself with his rag and lay down again. But this time, his feet were not covered. Ma offered pranaam, and then said to me, 'Charnon ki photo le le.' (Take a photo of his feet.)

Those were the days of analogue cameras and printing photos took time. When I received the prints nearly a month later, the man's feet were identical to those of Baba Maharaj.

Figure in the woods, en route to Poornagiri

In those days, on mountain routes, the Brahmin priests would provide small huts on the way for pilgrims to take rest or spend the night. These clearings would be called 'padaav-s'. After walking the whole day, as it began to get dark, we neared a padaav, Tuniyas. Everyone began to discuss arrangements for the night. As if drawn to something, Ma simply entered a hut. We followed her. She stated that this was where we would spend the night.

It was pitch-dark inside. Soon, the pandit, who was called Mathur Da, came running in with a lantern in his hand. In the flickering light cast by the flame, we saw a big murti of Hanuman ji by the mud wall.

That night, we ate simple aloo rasa with rotis for dinner. Even though it was December, what was unforgettable was that the sabji was so hot with chillis, that we broke into a sweat that cold winter night. Two coarse black blankets were provided to each of us as bedding. All the ladies slept in a row in that hut, with Ma and Chhoti Mataji on one side. The next morning, we bathed in the bracing water of the mountain spring and resumed our trek.

Ma and I walked ahead and reached the temple steps before the others. The improvised stairs were hewed out of the rocks in the mountain. A little before we reached the shrine, Ma decided to wait for Chhoti Ma. It was a calm and peaceful morning. The sky was a deep blue, and the sunlight filtered in through the trees. As we sat there, I heard the conch and the sounds of bells, amidst chants. Hearing these familiar sounds, I presumed there must be a crowd of pilgrims up at the shrine. I remembered that since the temple was situated at the top of the mountain peak, the little courtyard in front of the shrine was very small. I thought it would be best to wait till the people in the temple came down.

Presently, Chhoti Ma joined us with the rest of our group, and we climbed the final few steps. Reaching the temple, I was astounded to see that it was completely empty. There were no pilgrims there—not even the pujari. I was taken aback, wondering where the auspicious sounds had come from.[2]

Meanwhile, Ma went ahead to the small shrine and offered pranaam by putting her head to the ground. When she rose, I observed that on her forehead was the customary 'tilak' of vermilion sandal paste, grains of rice and a tulsi leaf. I took a photograph and captured the moment.

*

After Ma's mahasamadhi and the completion of Ma's temples in Kainchi and Rishikesh, I made a pilgrimage to Poornagiri. Ma had taken me to the Devi all those years ago, and I felt it was for me a silent initiation into the new life that was to begin. I went to offer my gratitude to Poornagiri Devi for having blessed me with thirty-seven years of sublime and blissful life at the feet of Ma.

---

[2] In popular practice, bells, gongs and cymbals are used to invoke gods and spiritual entities.

I visited the dak bungalow in Boom. Everything had changed. A modern structure had replaced the old rest house. There was now a well-planned garden instead of a forest-like grove. But the well from which I had drawn water for Ma was still there. I drank from it. Then I walked to the riverbed. The same rocks, the water flowing gently, and the setting sun.

I could see her footprints on the sands of time.

Chapter 12

In Kakrighat, 22 kilometres down the road from Kainchi and almost halfway to Almora, is perhaps the most beautiful murti of Sri Hanuman ji, installed and consecrated by Baba Maharaj in the year 1965. The Kakrighat Temple is situated on the bank of the Kosi river. As in Kainchi, the river in front of the temple has a northward flow, and is known as the Uttarvahini Ganga.

Kakrighat was a resting place for pilgrims going to Badrinath on foot over a hundred years ago, and a narrow steel bridge still exists—in a dilapidated state—to tell the story of their crossing the river here, before ascending to higher altitudes. Kakrighat has also been a tapo bhoomi[1] of many saints and sages in the past, and perhaps it was for this reason that Maharaj ji chose to sanctify the place by making a temple here.

A few landmarks still exist, bearing testimony to the sacredness of Kakrighat. The renowned saint of Kumaon, Somvar Giri Baba, lived here. The Shiv linga worshipped by

---

[1] A place where spiritual austerities are performed by saints.

him is in a temple under the banyan tree. The place where he cooked his simple meals—surrounded by a circular wall made of rocks and stones—has been preserved as it was. This is where he used to make khichdi, and feed the hundreds who came to him. The village elders went on to tell us that Somvar Giri Baba would stay in Kakrighat in the hot summer months and proceed to Padampuri for the icy cold winters, making a halt in the woods of Kainchi, in the cave behind the Hanuman Temple.

Nearby is a small mud hut with a slate roof, over five hundred years old, in which lived Gudri Baba. Also in the vicinity are three samadhis of sages who, having reached the highest transcendental state in their spiritual quest, discarded their mortal forms here at their own will. Two other names mentioned by the village elders were Trishool and Nishankh, the wandering siddhas who would frequent Kakrighat.

My first visit to Kakrighat with Ma dates to the beginning of the 1980s. I had observed that when Kainchi got very intense with too many visitors, Ma would suddenly leave the ashram for Kakrighat or elsewhere. She would say 'chal' with a snap of her finger—something I had come to read as a sign of urgency—and, in no time, we would be on our way.

On one such day, in the late afternoon, Ma and Chhoti Mataji decided to leave for Kakrighat, accompanied by one of the Mai-s and myself. In those days, the new bridge across the river had not yet been constructed. The car had to be left on the main road, near a few huts and tea shops, and we crossed the river on the old bridge and walked to the temple. The local people, few in number, were delighted to see the mothers, and they helped with the baggage, which consisted mainly of our beddings.

By the river, between two mountain ranges, nestled the small temple with the large murti of Hanuman ji. The ashram comprised three tiny rooms, with almost pigeonhole windows. Ma stayed in the first room, barely 8 by 8 feet in size. The next room was for those accompanying Ma; and in the last one lived the pujari, Siyaram Baba. There was no electricity, and no toilets either, and one had to resort to the river and the woods for natural needs.

Siyaram ji, overjoyed at the arrival of the mothers, rushed to prepare some tea and light the kerosene lanterns. It was going to be dark soon. Ma and Chhoti Mataji sat in the open verandah on their usual seat of a folded blanket, surrounded by the village elders. Trilok da, Jas da, Than Singh and a few others gathered around her. As I cleaned Ma's room, I enjoyed listening to the conversation that ensued between Ma and the old men. Speaking in Kumaoni, Ma greeted them in an endearingly familiar way, 'Kas hairo cha? Nantin kas chan?' (How have you been? How are the children?) They told her about their crops, the poor yield that year, their aches and pains, their truant sons, and how hard life was in general.

Meanwhile, Siyaram ji had lit a dhuni for Ma. I remember, after the elders left, the four of us—myself, Siyaram ji and the two mothers—sat till late in the verandah that night, with the lantern flickering in one corner.

Ma spoke of the day when Hanuman ji's murti was carried across the river for consecration, of how hundreds of monkeys had appeared as though to witness the occasion. She went on to tell me about the two large banyan trees, one in front of us and the other a little distance away, behind the temple. One, she said, was in a feminine form and bore the seeds, whereas the other, the male form, had 'jataas' and bore no fruit. Siyaram Baba then told us that he had heard from his forefathers that an old couple did tapasya in Kakrighat, and the two banyan trees sprouted after they left their mortal forms.

Siyaram ji brought hot milk for the mothers and me. After that, Ma retired to her kuti. A few minutes later, calling from inside, she said that I should sleep in the same room as her. I had already made two beds on the floor for both the mothers and there was barely any extra space. By the time I went in, Ma had squeezed the bedding to make place for me. Soon after, the mothers were asleep.

As I lay awake, the thought crossed my mind that Ma might need to go out at night, and she would need help. I quietly tied a corner of her dhoti to the buttonhole of my kurta. It must have been well past midnight when I felt a tug on my shirt.

I woke up and saw Ma sitting cross-legged, looking out through the open door at the banyan tree. I, too, sat up behind her and was amazed at what I saw. It seemed as though, in that dark night, a thousand lamps had been lit. Such was the radiance outside that I could clearly see the leaves, the branches of the tree and all else around it. Very gradually, the glow faded. This was followed by the sound of many bells and drums which rose in a crescendo and then slowly merged into the silence of the night.

Ma turned to look at me and I gathered the courage to ask her what it was that I saw and heard. Ma said, 'Jab sant chalta hai to aisa hi prakash hota hai. Ghant-nagaro ki dhwani hoti hai.' (When a saint walks, there is such illumination. The sounds of bells and drums are heard.)

*

Over the years, Ma would often spend the entire month of Kartik, which falls around November, in Kakrighat. Time would slow down for all of us here. Kartik being the most auspicious month of the Hindu calendar, we would all immerse ourselves in our own spiritual observances. During these stays, there would be day visits to Jageshwar, to the Gola Devta in Chitai and the Gananath Temple near Satrali. Once, Ma expressed a desire to visit the temples in Almora, and it was then that I saw many of the temples that Ma would often reminiscence about. The Ragunath Mandir, the Murli Manohar Mandir— her childhood playground—the Hanuman Mandir, the Ashta Bhairav Temple, Badrinath Mandir, to name a few. Also, the Khutkuni Bhairav Temple, which was close to where Chhoti Mataji had lived and loved going to as a child.

In Kakrighat, both the mothers would take snaan in the river anytime between 3 a.m. and 4 a.m. Accompanied by another person, I would run down the steps with mothers' clothes and a lantern, to a particular place by the river where the water was shallow. Both mothers would bathe here. Close to the river, there was a willow-like tree with a low-stooping branch. I would use it as a hanger for their clothes and for the lantern. Having done this, we would return to the temple.

One morning, Ma had descended the steps almost halfway, followed by Chhoti Mataji, when we met them on our way up. All of a sudden, we heard the roars of a tiger echoing in the valley. Siyaram Baba came out of his kuti and rushed down with his trishul.[2] Ma stopped him. Then, she clapped her hands thrice. The sharp sound of the clap pierced through the valley. We waited a while. There was complete silence. Then Ma proceeded to bathe in the river.

Often, both mothers would go to the Bhairavnath Mandir which was at a little distance from the temple. Here was the peepal tree, under which Swami Vivekananda had his first experience of samadhi. Close to it was the cremation ground, with a small hut, in which lived an old man who would come out as soon as he saw Ma. Ma addressed him as Hari Bhagat and he, in turn, would call her Gayatri Mata. His entire conversation with Ma was through impromptu songs, in which he would mimic the music of a stringed instrument. Ma seemed to enjoy it. Sometimes, before leaving, she would slip off her shawl and put it over Hari Bhagat's shoulders. So deftly was this done that I did not notice it until later.

There is a small kuti with a slate roof just above the Hanuman mandir. Often, Ma and Chhoti Mataji would spend

---

[2] Trident.

Ma and Jivanti mataji in Kakrighat, under the peepal tree where Swami
Vivekananda experienced Samadhi

the morning there, sitting in the little courtyard. Ma told me
about two old women who lived there many years ago. They
would say that sometimes they saw a very tall monkey, wearing
a red loin cloth, carrying two little bhaus, baby boys, on
his shoulders. At other times they would see four little boys
crawling in the courtyard. It was believed that the monkey was
Hanuman ji and the little boys were Sri Ram and his three
brothers. Reminding us of the blessing conferred on Hanuman
ji by Sri Sita ji, Ma would say, 'Hanuman ji ajar, amar hain.'[3]

*

---

[3] Lord Hanuman is blessed with eternal youth and immortality.

Ma with Hari Bhagat in Kakrighat

This holy place watched over by Hanuman ji himself remains as pristine today as it was in those early years when I first travelled there with Ma. Further enhancing the spiritual energy of Kakrighat, there is now a small temple for Maharaj ji there. In 2008, the murti that was brought to Kakrighat from Veerapuram in Chennai—as per Ma's wishes—was ceremoniously installed in the temple that adjoins Hanuman ji's mandir, amid great celebrations. A big bhandara was organized on this occasion. Maharaj ji's murti is made of black stone, dressed in a blanket and dhoti of the sort he used to wear.

A couple of years later, there was a cloudburst in Kumaon. In the resulting devastation, Somvar Giri Baba's small temple below the banyan tree was washed away, and the Shivling was completely submerged. When the water receded, Ma went to Kakrighat, and though the pujaris had cleaned the space somewhat, all around were the debris that had collected during the flood: animal carcasses, torn clothes and shoes, pieces of wood, other waste. Deeply pained, Ma turned to the devotees who were accompanying us, and said that the Shivling, which had not moved at all during the catastrophe, should still be placed at a higher level now, and a new temple should be constructed for it.

Chapter 13

Ma usually left Kainchi in the third week of June for ekaantvaas, bringing in a period of rest and recuperation for all of us. During these retreats, time would slow down, and our tired minds would awaken to nature and its scenic beauty. The mothers too were relieved of the relentless commitments they had at the ashram in Kainchi.

During ekaantvaas, every morning Ma would go for long walks in the woods, and it would be such a pleasure to accompany her as she picked wildflowers, showed me herbs in the mountains and told me about their curative values. Often, we would pass a small temple dedicated to a local deity. This would invariably become a resting point. Ma would choose a rock to sit on, and tell me about the deities of the Kumaon hills as well as stories of her childhood and later life. It was here that I was allowed free play with my camera, and I had the best opportunity to photograph Ma.

One year in the late 1980s, the mothers' departure on the ekaantvaas was delayed. Ma had decided to stay on as she felt the winding up of the ashram after the June bhandara needed her presence. However, this meant that instead of people gradually vacating the ashram, fresh arrivals began, with people pouring in.

Ma decided the only way to ease the situation would be for her to move on to the summer retreat—to her ekaantvaas—because as soon as the news of Ma's departure would spread, the number of visitors would begin to dwindle; life in Kainchi would slow down, the ashram could be taken care of and the staff, who had been overworked by now, could take turns to go home for short breaks.

Ma called some of us—the office bearers, me and the few who would be accompanying her—and told to get ready as she would like to leave early next morning. We were all taken aback as no prior arrangements for their stay had been made as yet. Every single one of us was concerned, and apprising her of the predicament, we requested for a few days to organize everything, make the usual travel arrangements, and so on. Ma was firm on her decision. In a quiet moment, I asked her where we would be going. Ma cut me short, saying, 'We will go wherever Maharaj ji will take us.'

We left early as planned. This time a second car from the ashram escorted my car, with the mothers, as everyone wanted to ensure Ma's safe arrival wherever she chose to go. It was an unusual drive, stopping at every turn or crossroad, and waiting for Ma to tell me which way to go. Making a halt at every sight of civilization, the men in our group who were following us, would go and look for suitable accommodation or a dak bungalow for

Ma's stay. We crossed Almora, drove on to Berinaag, and from there to Chaukori. It was past 5 p.m., and all our efforts had been futile so far. Soon it would be dark and having driven all day, fatigue and anxiety showed on our faces as we secretly worried about where the mothers would stay the night.

In sheer desperation, we even went to check out a government rest house, but it turned out to be rather unsuitable. Ma called me to her car then and said that there was a Hanuman temple a few kilometres ahead of Chaukori in Kotmanya, and the pandit, Ishwari Dutt, was a devotee of Maharaj ji. Ma said we should go there.

The distance was about 20 kilometres and we reached Kotmanya in no time. It was a very remote area, and I could see no hill house or construction of any kind except two tiny shops by the roadside, which were cemented structures. I still remember that one was a small grocery shop, while the other sold tea and samosas. A little ahead, I observed a small temple, where it seemed some celebration was taking place. Village women in colourful sarees, a few men in kurtas and dhotis, and many children had gathered there. As soon as our car approached the temple, the excitement heightened.

As I slowed the car, a small Tibetan rug was quickly unrolled, the wicks of the lamps were lit by the women, and a scramble commenced to be in front. When Ma alighted, arati was done to her amidst singing, accompanied by the sacred sounds of conches, gongs and bells. It was such a beautiful welcome for Ma. The mothers, perfectly at ease, sat in the temple—the women and the children crowding over them.

I was thoroughly confused. None of us knew where we were going until we arrived in Kotmanya. And here, they were saying that they had been waiting for us since the morning. Curiosity got the better of me. I took Ishwari Dutt ji aside and asked him if he had any prior information about Ma's arrival. He smiled, almost with a sense of pride, and said that Maharaj ji had come to him in a dream the night before. He told him that both mothers would be coming to Kotmanya in the morning. He should make arrangements for their stay. Ishwari Dutt went on to say that Maharaj ji had also said, 'Do takhat laga dena!' (Have two cots laid out!)

After a very refreshing ginger tea was served to us in steel glasses—in the traditional pahaadi way—at the temple, we drove back to where the two shops stood. A few steps led down from the verandah. Walking down, we came to two simple rooms. One had been provided with two beds and a schoolroom desk. I was so relieved to see this spartan but ideal setting, almost perfect for the mothers, right next to the little window from where the mothers had a beautiful view of the valley below, and the small desk where Ma would write Ram-naam. In the other room, the rest of our party settled down for the night, and we managed to improvise a kitchen in one corner. Chapatis and a sabzi were cooked and bhog was offered to Maharaj ji's blanket. The next morning, the men who had accompanied us left for Kainchi.

The next three weeks were spent in the lap of nature. Gentle undulating meadows, lush with green grass, lay on all sides. Beautiful waterfalls gushed down the hillside, and this was where we took our baths every day. I remember sitting on a rock one day with the mothers and suddenly hearing a bubbling sound. Looking for the source, we found that a little spring had broken forth from the earth and was now rippling out from beneath the rock.

In the surrounding forests were little pathways and clearings, where the mothers liked to walk in the woods. Ma would pick wildflowers and make tiny little bouquets, she would point out herbs in the mountains and tell me about their curative values. Often, we would go past small enclosures erected with a few slabs of stone which were dedicated to local deities. Then the mothers would tell me about the devis and the devatas of the Kumaon hills. I loved taking photographs here. Often on these walks, we were joined by the women of the village, who conversed with the mothers in their naturally unpretentious way. They would open their hearts to the mothers about their daily household matters: the cow wasn't giving milk, a grandchild was ill, the harvest was poor. The mothers would give them gentle guidance.

In the evenings, after dinner prasad, I would read to both mothers from old issues of the *Kalyan* magazine, which was published by Gita Press Gorakhpur and a household fixture in those days. There was always a chapter called 'Bhakta Gatha' about the life of some saint, and both mothers loved hearing these.

Even though we had brought some supplies with us, for the perishables we were dependent on a truck with supplies that would come to the hillside once a week. Since there was no other traffic plying on that road, I still remember we could hear the truck from far away, and by the time it arrived, the entire village would be on the road. We bought potatoes, sugar, jaggery, locally grown pears and apples. The women in the village would send their children in the mornings with milk, curd and vegetables, especially fresh cucumbers and corn cobs, from their backyards. We didn't want for anything.

*

When Guru Purnima was nearing, Ma said it was time for us to return to Kainchi. She chose a date for our departure. As always, this was in July, and by now the monsoons were here. There was a sudden outbreak of intense rain in Kotmanya. The villagers told us that overnight the hill road had been severely damaged, and a part of it—about a 20 feet stretch—had sunk into a chasm, making it impossible for vehicles to commute back and forth. Two of us walked to the site and saw the huge gap between two ends of the road. This could only be bridged when the rain stopped.

Around midday, members of Ishwari's family told us the following story. A marriage party had arrived in a bus from Pankhu, which lay ahead of Kotmanya. Naturally, they were very eager to make the onward journey so as not to miss the auspicious time for the wedding. They summoned the villagers, and paying them a generous sum of money, they asked the young men amongst them to fill the gorge with rocks and boulders. A large group of men got together, and it took them four to five hours to fill the gap. The bus was able to pass through. Having crossed, they stopped again, and promised some more money to the villagers, requesting the elders to maintain the road till their return the day after.

We packed up and left Kotmanya the next morning, reaching Kainchi well in time for Guru Purnima.

Chapter 14

In the summer of 1988, Ma travelled to the small Himalayan town of Chakrata, about 100 kilometres from Dehradun, on her ekaantvaas. Situated between the rivers Ton and Yamuna, Chakrata was a beautiful town, nestled among conifers, rhododendrons and birches, 7000 feet above sea-level. Jhaldiyal ji, a senior officer in the State Government, had the forest guest house reserved for the mothers. He personally came on the day of our departure and escorted Ma's car to Chakrata. The official cars led the way. We followed.

For the most part, the day was bright and sunny, with panoramic views of the mountains. On the way, as we neared Bairat khai, known as the princess of the hills for its picturesque beauty, the weather changed suddenly. There was a heavy downpour. Visibility was almost nil because of the thick fog and the cars were crawling with their headlights turned on. The challenge came when we reached a part of the road with brown muddy slush, no parapets to mark the edges, and deep gorges on both sides. Grim murmurs of the Hanuman Chalisa could be heard from the back seat. I thanked God for a vehicle with a four-wheel drive.

Slowly, we made our way up the treacherous slope, reaching Chakrata by late afternoon. The place had served as a cantonment of the British Indian army, who occupied the town as early as 1869. The dak bungalow was a typical colonial structure, a beautiful house with wooden floors, arched windows with tinted glass panes, hanging lights and fireplaces. But time had taken its toll. The doors were creaky, the furniture seemed jittery, and dust covered every surface. In front of the house were beautiful trees, rhododendrons and palms, with clusters of hydrangeas flowering in an unkempt garden.

As in most hill houses, the bedrooms were on the first floor. The day was getting on, so the five of us cleaned the room that had been set aside for the mothers. Having done this, a little Ganga water was sprinkled around. Guggul dhoop was put in a fire that had been lit in an old cauldron. A small puja altar was set up on a table and Maharaj ji's blanket duly placed on it. Once this was done, both the mothers went inside to rest.

Now it was our turn. As we were cleaning the place, every one of us had the sense that there was something not quite right about the house. By now it was pitch dark outside. One by one we shared our feelings, and then it was decided that instead of occupying the bedrooms in the house, we would organize our beddings in the lounge, turning it into a dormitory of sorts. Sharad, the only young man in our group, and our helper boy Heera chose the landing to sleep on. Already, there was talk of the eerie: 'Who banged on the door?' None of us did. 'Where did the matchbox go?' No one took it. Odd little things were happening around us, but we did not pay too much heed to them. After taking dinner prasad and ensuring that both the mothers were comfortable, we offered our pranaams to them and retired to the adjoining room to sleep.

A little past midnight, we were woken up by the clear sound of footsteps that could be heard on the tin roof of the verandah that was just outside our window. It was accompanied by the jingling sound of anklets, the kind that hill women wear. None of us dared to get up and look out. I peeped into Ma's room. Both mothers were awake. We remained huddled up in our beds. Apart from a few snatches of sleep now and then, it seemed like a very long night, broken intermittently by the footsteps and the jingling anklets.

At morning tea, we shared the night's happenings with Ma. Both mothers said that they too had heard the sounds and were unable to sleep at night. Ma said, 'Yahan kisi ki adhogati hui hai. Kisi ki atma mukt hone ke liye bhatak rahi hai.' (Someone has died an unnatural death and the soul is seeking liberation.)

When we were done with our morning routine and prayers, Ma called the watchman and asked him to bring a few elderly men living nearby. After many denials, they came out with the story that way back when the British garrison was stationed here, a local woman committed suicide by jumping from the roof due to the oppressive behaviour of an officer. They ultimately confessed that they too see an apparition of a woman and hear similar sounds. They said this has been happening for many years and though her spirit haunts the house, we need not be afraid as she was a harmless soul. None of us dared to speak, but in our hearts, we all wished that Ma would ask us to simply pack up and leave. Ma said no such thing.

We returned to the house and Ma asked us to place our puja books, especially the Ramayana and the Srimad Bhagvat on each windowsill. Heera Singh prepared a coal fire and put handfuls of Guggul dhoop into it, almost filling the entire house with the smoke. Then commenced a marathon of prayers. Ma said we should begin akhand paath, or continuous recitation of the Ramayana for three days. We all took turns. Both mothers would also read in the mornings. This went on day and night. The nocturnal sounds faded away and the air felt as though washed and cleaned. We were able to settle into that house and everything returned to normal.

Soon it was July. After a few days, the monsoons broke. There was torrential rain in those parts, which continued unabated for more than a week. All of a sudden, one evening Ma said she would like to leave for Kainchi the very next morning. Our only window to the world outside was a small tea shop near the guest house, with some basic supplies. The man at the shop informed us that a large part of the road near Kalsi had been completely washed away and it would be impossible for us to move out. The local people who had been trying to walk across had slipped on the hillside, and a few had even lost their lives. We went back to Ma and apprised her of the situation, suggesting that we stay on for a few more days. I tried my best, but Ma remained adamant and insisted we leave the next day.

In that incessant rain, Sharad and Heera loaded the baggage, and we left around 10 in the morning, late by Ma's standards. As we drove past the grocer's shop, he signalled at us frantically, telling us not to go. There was no sign of life on the road—just rain and gushing waterfalls—and the car had to almost wade through the water.

Not far from Kalsi, we arrived at the point where the road had been damaged. A few army jeeps and trucks had been lined up, and many men in their service uniforms and rain gear could be seen. We were told to park our car on one side. One of the personnel walked up to us and informed us that the soldiers had been deployed to cut into the hillside and provide a track for the General's car as he needed to get to Dehradun urgently. He advised me to line up behind the army vehicles as the track would be closed soon after the General passed by. We waited, and when the General's convoy moved, we followed the army trucks. Ours was the only civilian car to pass through, as the improvised road was closed soon after.

I remember the tremendous sense of relief after crossing over. Haridwar was still some distance away and we would have to stop here for the night. It was a difficult situation as it would be dark by the time we reached there. None of us knew of an ashram or dharamshala appropriate for the mothers to stay. Hotels were unthinkable.

I expressed my concern to Ma. A while later, a policeman on a motorcycle followed by a pilot car stopped all the traffic on the road. I too parked the jeep on one side. We were told to clear the road as the chief minister was passing by. Soon, a fleet of cars went past us. One of the cars at the back suddenly stopped, and I heard a loud 'Jai Ma!' I saw Mr Jhaldiyal almost jump out from his seat. He was on official duty and delighted to see Ma. After he had offered his salutations, I did not waste time and asked him to suggest an appropriate place for Ma to stay in Haridwar. Mr Jhaldiyal said he had booked an apartment in the newly constructed Jai Ram Ashram, overlooking the Ganga, for the chief minister, but his programme had been cancelled at the last minute, and he was proceeding directly to Dehradun. The accommodation was lying vacant. Jhaldiyal ji himself led Ma's car to Haridwar. The rooms were simple and spotless, and since cleanliness was the prime requisite for the mothers, it suited our requirements perfectly.

And so, we ended up spending four very pleasant days in Haridwar. In the mornings we took Ganga snaan, while in the evenings, we would sit in a balcony facing Ganga ji and do our prayers.

One evening, the two ladies accompanying Ma were busy in the kitchen, and Sharad had gone to the market for supplies. That left me alone with the mothers and I somehow felt self-conscious singing the prarthna all by myself. I started with the prayers. After a few minutes, a beautiful male voice accompanied my singing. Taking for granted that Sharad was back, I felt easy and continued without looking back. After the prayers, as I offered pranaam to her, Ma asked, 'Who was singing with you?'

I confessed that since I am not a singer, I was happy that Sharad had joined us. Ma said, 'Where is Sharad? Call him.'

I couldn't find him and so went to the kitchen. The ladies there said he was not back from the market yet. I came back and told Ma that Sharad was not there, but I had heard someone sing along with me. Ma told me to go and check all the four rooms on our floor. There was no one in the three rooms, but in the fourth one, which was Ma's room, there was an exceptionally oversized monkey comfortably seated on the windowsill. When I told Ma of this, she asked for a mango, and told me to offer it as prasad to the monkey and offer him salutations from afar.

Chapter 15

I remember Ma saying that years ago, Maharaj ji had once sent a murti of Hanuman ji with a few devotees and asked them to build a temple for him in Pauri. In those days, Pauri was a small town in the Garhwal hills. For whatever reasons, the temple did not get made, and after Maharaj ji's mahasamadhi, the matter was almost forgotten. Except, of course, by Ma. Ma had several letters sent to devotees in Pauri to enquire about the whereabouts of the murti. After a great deal of effort, she came to know that it was in the Kyunkaleshwar Temple, a famous Shiva temple in Pauri, dating back to the eighth century. And in the summer of 1989, accompanied by a small group of people from Kainchi, the mothers went to Pauri to look for the murti.

I remember the day we reached Pauri vividly. Ma received an enchanting welcome from the gods of weather. As she stepped down from the car, the sun shone bright upon her, even though there was a gentle shower falling on the mountains. The clear blue sky had a rainbow painted across the horizon.

To complete this picture, at that very moment we heard the sounds of chanting from a distant temple.

After a day or two, we went to the Kyunkaleshwar Temple. About 5 kilometres from Pauri town, amidst thick forests, stood this temple, built in the traditional Garhwali style of architecture. Lord Shiva is the presiding deity. It is believed that Yamraj, the god of death, worshipped Him here. After darshan of the temple deities, we began our search for Hanuman ji. On questioning the priests there, we were told that there was a murti in a kuti near the temple, in which a sadhu was living. Led by one of them, we walked to the tiny quarters.

In a small narrow room—so dark inside that a candle had to be lit—the murti was found in a corner. It was covered with dust. Rats had made a mess all around. The mothers sat on one side while we cleaned up the cave-like space. Once we finished, in that faint candlelight, we were able to see that it was a beautifully carved murti, made of red stone. Ma had come to the end of a very long search. We returned from Kyunkaleshwar with a sense of deep satisfaction.

In Pauri, we were staying in a traditional Garhwali cottage that belonged to Mr Jhaldiyal. Such was the location of the little house that the small windows opened to panoramic views of Himalayan peaks, from Panchachuli and Nanda Devi to Badri, Kedar and Kailash. That night, I remember the mothers slept very late, speculating about a suitable location for the temple.

The very next morning, Mr Jhaldiyal came over and requested Ma to accept a piece of land on his ancestral

property, just above the cottage we were in, for Hanuman ji. Ma said yes.

*

The temple came up in July 1992, and a bhandara was held in celebration. The Kainchi devotees had travelled up for the occasion, and the local people participated in large numbers. Hanuman ji was brought from Kyunkaleshwar to the new temple in a ceremonial procession, with devotees walking joyfully as they sang bhajans. Once again, I witnessed how Ma fulfilled Maharaj ji's sankalp.

After the temple was built, Ma would travel to Pauri every year. In time, Jhaldiyal ji had the cottage renovated for the mothers, and I have some of the most endearing memories of our stays there.

Above the little house was a reserved forest, with a beautiful road running by its side. Perhaps the best part of our stay in Pauri were the long morning walks with Ma and Chhoti Mataji. To not only see Ma amidst the natural beauty of the mountains, free and unfettered by her commitments to the ashrams, but also to be with her in that time gave me a deeper perspective of her.

In those days, the bridge to Devprayag was under construction so there was no traffic on this route. Since we would be the only ones there, we soon developed a fond affinity for that road. We had our own preferred landmarks on the way—chosen parapets for the mothers to sit and enjoy the

Himalayan view, rocky platforms where we would enjoy apples which I cut and served on leaves, and a large rock from which grew drooping long grass that Ma named Rishi-Muni shila. It was a delight to see the mothers so carefree. They would sometimes lie down on the green grass and blend with nature in silence. Meanwhile, I would get some of my best opportunities to take their photographs.

One morning, Ma came out alone, saying that Jivanti Mataji would not be accompanying us on the walk that day. I noticed that she was sniffling and wiping her nose. The weather had suddenly changed the previous night. It was unusually cold, and perhaps she had caught a chill. I tried to suggest that it was not the best weather for going out and maybe we should

Morning walks in the hills of Pauri

just stay in, but Ma walked on silently. I had no choice but to follow her!

I was surprised when she suddenly asked me if I had been to Bubakhaal. I told her that I had heard that Bubakhaal was a small hamlet about 6 kilometres away, but I'd had no reason to visit the place. Ma, a habitual fast walker, picked up pace. Climbing up the hill, we reached the forest road. I kept up with her.

We had barely walked for about ten minutes when suddenly, Ma stopped. Turning towards me, she said in a very casual way, 'Tu yeh mat kehna tune kabhi sher nahin dekha.' (Don't tell me you have never seen a tiger.) She then held my hand in hers and pointed to a thick cluster of trees. In the dense forest, amid the foliage, was a huge tiger, its skin flamboyant orange with the conspicuous black stripes. The tiger was at a distance of about 15 metres and, luckily, its back was towards us. I asked Ma to return immediately, but she said, 'No, the animal seems in an angry mood. We should walk on.' I was petrified! Going ahead on a winding road with many turns and a tiger lurking in the area! It was a dangerous predicament, to say the least.

We had walked on for a little distance when Ma told me to wait there. She said she would go back and take a look from the bend to check if the animal could still be seen. Before I could stop her, Ma had walked back. She was out of my sight for what must have been a few seconds, but for me, it felt like an eternity. She returned saying, 'Voh sadak par aa gaya hai. Jaldi chal.' (The tiger has come on to the road. Come, we must go quickly now.) Ma grabbed me by my upper arm, and almost as if dragging a stubborn child, she doubled her pace, and we walked on. It seemed like an endless trek! We must have covered a few kilometres when we met a forest guard.

Aware of the danger, he ran up to us and warned that there was a tigress in the forest. He said that she was in a rage as her cubs had been killed the night before. He went on to say that until she avenges their death with a kill, she will not calm down, and so we should walk as fast as possible. We trudged for what seemed like a long distance, till we reached a point where the road forked in two directions. There were a couple of shacks on the hillside, and a few men were working on the road. Tired out, Ma and I sat down under the shade of a tree. I asked one of the men the name of the place. They told me that it was Bubakhaal. Just before we had commenced on our walk that morning, Ma had asked me if I had been to Bubakhaal!

I enquired from the men if it was possible to get some sort of conveyance to take us home. They told me that no vehicles went that way because the bridge was under construction and the road was closed. The only way, they said, was to go to Pauri town and get a taxi from there. This meant a walk of another few kilometres. Ma began to express concern that Chhoti Mataji would worry as we were normally back much sooner on other days. With my thoughts in a quandary, I did not know what to do. Just then, I saw a white Ambassador car at a distance, coming towards us. I quickly stepped onto the road and waved at the car to stop. Even before I could speak, the driver, without looking at me, shook his head. He then pointed his thumb backwards to say he was not going ahead, but in the direction from which Ma and I had come. I told him we lived on that very side and asked if we could go with him. Again, with his eyes averted, he nodded in assent. I quickly helped Ma into the car and got in myself.

I was overwhelmed by a tremendous sense of relief to be safely on our way home. As I sat back, a peculiar thought crossed my mind that the driver's head from the back was exactly like Baba's. After a while, I told him that there was a small Hanuman temple ahead and we would like to get off there. He gave a strange reply, saying, 'Inko to main jaanta hoon. Inki janam bhoomi toh Almora hai.' (I know her. Her birthplace is Almora.) I was perplexed on hearing this, but there was no time to think further as we had reached the temple gate and the car stopped there. Ma told me to run down the hill and get some money to give to the driver. Walking down, I looked back with a little bit of concern and saw Ma talking to him. Then, I saw that she folded her hands, and bowing a little, she offered pranaam to him. The 'driver' placed his hand on her head to bless her. Then he got into the car and sped off straight ahead. Where could he go? The road was closed as there was no bridge.

Ma returned to the house, but I kept a silent watch, waiting for the car to return.

No car came back.

Chapter 16

Cascading down the hills, the Ganges flows into the small town of Rishikesh, where the very air is perfumed by the breath of the river goddess. The gateway to the shrines of Badri and Kedarnath, Gangotri and Yamunotri, Rishikesh bears an aura of profound spirituality. There are indelible memories from childhood that cling to my mind: bathing in the Ganga, saffron-clad sadhus on pilgrimage, the large crowds at Har Ki Pauri and visits to the old ashrams. The most vivid of these were frequent darshans of the great saint, Swami Sivananda Maharaj, at the Sivananda Ashram. Swami ji used to give cashews for prasad, and I called him 'Kaaju wale baba'. As I write this, I offer salutations to him.

In the year 1970, land had been obtained by Maharaj ji in Rishikesh for making a Hanuman temple. After his mahasamadhi, it fell into neglect, and over the years, the plot came to be occupied by local people. Through Ma's perseverance and with her blessings, the land was reclaimed and in 1984, Ma had a small murti of Hanuman ji installed in a modest temple with a tin roof. From then onwards, the two mothers would visit Rishikesh almost every second month. After Kainchi, it became a second home to us. A simple hut with a thatched roof and wood pillars was made, where Ma would meet all the visitors and devotees. She would stay in a tent. Some distance away, a row of tents was pitched for the others with a provisional tin shed kitchen. Looking back now, the premises seemed more like a safari camp than an ashram.

Soon after, the ashram came alive with recitations of the Ramayana, verily the Sunderkand, and of course the Hanuman Chalisa. A simple brick wall was erected to enclose the area, and Kamal, the night watchman, would pass the night writing Ram Ram on each brick with a piece of chalk. In a few years, a beautiful temple came up at the same spot. Suggestions poured in that a larger murti of Hanuman ji in marble should replace the old one. Ma answered them, saying, 'Yeh pratishith vigrah hai. Hanuman ji khilona nahin hai. Yehi pooji hui murti hai. Yehi rahegi.' (This murti has been consecrated. Hanuman ji is not a toy. This murti has been worshipped. It will remain.)

Once, Maharaj ji had said to a mason, Sri Ram, that one day there would be a forty-seven feet tall murti of Hanuman ji in Rishikesh. He had added, 'Unko ooper dekhoge to tumhari topi gir jayegi.' (Your cap will fall off when you look up at him!) Sri Ram used to wear a Gandhi cap on his head.

The words of Maharaj ji were a holy testament to Ma, and she brought even his most abstract thoughts to life.

And so, a forty-seven feet tall murti of Hanuman ji was made, and it is a landmark of Rishikesh today. All pilgrims coming from Haridwar pause for his darshan before proceeding on their onward journey to the mountains.

*

As Ma's bond with Rishikesh grew deeper, her visits became more frequent. I would drive the mothers from Kainchi, and it became a little ritual for us to stop at a dilapidated little temple, near Kashipur, to refresh ourselves. Close to the temple was a large peepal tree, a mud platform running around it. The two mothers used to lie down on the platform and relax awhile, and the rest of us would sit around. One day, Ma told me that once Maharaj ji's temple has been built, we will put a small murti of Hanuman ji here.

In time, a temple for Maharaj ji was envisioned by Ma. The mothers would now travel frequently to Jaipur. Ma would herself sit in the murti bhandar for hours, checking the minutest details of the clay model. Later, when the marble was being sculpted, we would go to Jaipur again and spend the day in the murti emporium, surrounded by marble statues of all the gods and goddesses of the Hindu pantheon. The mothers would be seated in an adjoining room. When the sculptors would leave for a lunch break, Ma would take out Maharaj ji's blanket from the travel bag and cover the marble that was being sculpted with it till the men returned.

Finally, in 1997, Maharaj ji's temple was ready and the day for the prana pratishtha of his murti came. Preparations for the Vedic rituals had been made, and a particular hour was decided by the pandits for the placing of Maharaj ji's murti on the pedestal the next morning. That night, when all were asleep, Ma came out of her kuti at 2 a.m. and sent a word to the workers that the murti should be taken to the temple right away. The men got together, and the murti was carried the distance very carefully. Ma followed them. Pages of Ram-naam from Ma's notebooks were mixed with cement and mortar on the pedestal, and the murti was placed on it. Ganga water was sprinkled by Ma. The next day commenced the ceremonies, and bhandara and jubilation followed.

Remembering Ma's words to me at the Shiva Temple near Kashipur, I bought a stone murti of Hanuman ji for four hundred rupees—this I remember—and had it put in the mandir for consecration. The day we were returning, Ma told me to place the murti in the back seat of the car, between the two mothers, for the onward journey. Since it was a consecrated murti, Ma did not want me to pack it.

I still remember vividly that on reaching our destination, Ma carried the murti like a baby as she walked up to the temple, gently placing it in the centre of the puja. 'Inka naam hai pooran kaam Hanuman', she said. (His name is pooran kaam Hanuman.)

*

During the constructions of these temples, Ma would go to Rishikesh whenever she felt the call. It was nothing unusual for her to tell me in Kainchi, a night before, that we would be

Drives with Ma in the red Gypsy

leaving early the next day. These were short trips so I, a trained traveller by now, would pack a few essentials and leave Kanchi before daybreak—around 3 a.m. There would be no traffic on the road in the early hours and we would be in Rishikesh by 9 a.m.

I remember, on one occasion, after a week-long stay in Rishikesh, Ma told me that she would like to return to Kainchi the next morning. Since Rishikesh was the only place where we had access to a market for our personal needs, I went out to the bazaar and spent all of the little money I had on essentials. When I returned to the ashram, I was informed that there was a change in Ma's programme. Ma said that the finer details of the temples required her presence in Rishikesh, and she wishes to stay on.

My first thought was, 'No money, no cheque book!' Those were not the days of ATMs and Paytm-s. My most urgent need was to buy medicines for Chhoti Mataji as I had carried a limited supply, enough only for a short stay. That night, I could not sleep till late. Somehow, it did not feel right to borrow money, so I decided to sell my camera the next day. My pretext would be that I wanted to change it for a newer model.

I woke up a little past 4 a.m. and saw that both the mothers had gone to the temples. It was the month of December, making it cold and foggy outside. When Ma returned to the room, she told me that there was a sadhu in front of the Hanuman Temple. She asked me to take some tea from the kitchen and give it to him. Ma went on to add that he had a weird appearance, but I should not be scared. As I was leaving, Ma put her black blanket on my shoulder, asking me to give it to the sadhu, repeating once again, 'Tu darna mat.' (Do not be afraid.)

I took tea in a clay cup and went to the Hanuman Temple. A dark man with a cluster of unruly, long hair, and bare-chested, was lying on a heap of wet sand. Addressing him as Baba, I called out to him—saying Ma had sent tea for him. He got up and looked pleased. As he held the cup, I noticed he had exceptionally long nails, and on his finger was a metal band which was cutting into his flesh.

I asked him if it was hurting him and said, if he liked, I could help him slip it out with soap and hot water. He smiled and replied, 'Nahin, nahin, yeh to maine Shani ko pakad rakha hai.' (No, no, this is where I've kept Shani captive.) Sipping the tea, he began to speak, 'Tu yahin janam bhar seva karegi, gari bhi hogi, paisa bhi hoga, sab kuchh hoga, kabhi koi kami nahi hogi.' (This is where you will live and serve all your life, you will have a car, you will have money, and you will never be in want of anything.) I stood silent. After giving the blanket, I returned to Ma and gave her a verbatim account of what he had said. I noticed that both mothers seemed exceptionally happy this morning.

Soon I got busy with my routine and the events of the morning slipped out of my mind. In the afternoon, I quietly packed my camera and asked Ma if I could go to town. Ma seemed unwilling to let me go and delayed me by sending me on some errand or the other. Around teatime, at about 4 p.m., there was a knock on the door. I was told that a gentleman, well known to me, needed to see me urgently. As I stepped out, he came running towards me and said that he had come to Rishikesh on a business trip and was leaving for Nainital by the night bus. He said he had extra money in cash and wanted to know if I could bring it for him in the car, as he did not feel safe carrying it in the bus. I readily agreed. Handing me the packet, he ran for the waiting bus. I went into my room and unpacked my camera.

The same day, Dr Anoop, Ma's devotee, was on his way to Dehradun for a conference. He stopped on the way to stay a day in the ashram with Ma. After having given Chhoti mataji a check-up, he folded his hands, and with moist eyes, he said, 'Ma, I am your physician and also your son. I feel it is my duty to get your medicines. I have brought all the medicines

144

with me. I pray to you to please allow me this seva from now onwards.'

Later that night, when I was sitting with the mothers, Ma told me, 'Hanuman ji mein itni shakti hai ki woh Shani ko dabaa ke rakhte hain.' (Hanuman ji is so strong that he has the power to control the malefic influence of Saturn.) The words of the sadhu from that morning rang in my ears: 'Maine Shani ko pakad rakkhaa hai.'

*

As the years went by, Hanuman Jayanti came to be celebrated in a big way in Rishikesh with nine days of recitation of the Ramayana, and a large bhandara—where puri, aloo, kheer and laddus were fed to thousands. Rishikesh became the spiritual metropolis of all the devotees of Maharaj ji, who now looked to Ma. Easily accessible by road, rail and air, people could travel easily to Ma whenever she resided there. The simple, unostentatious love of the people of Rishikesh drew Ma to them. As soon as the word of her arrival spread, the ashram would begin filling up with devotees, and there would be a gentle tussle for darshan. Such was their yearning that Ma seemed to meet them with open arms.

As it would happen in Kainchi, the mothers would occasionally leave the Rishikesh ashram and spend a few quiet days near the Ganga. Sometimes, they would choose to stay by the Ganga for a week or more before going to the ashram. These decisions were spontaneous and intuitive. As per Ma's wish, their destination was not disclosed. Once, when we were driving down from Kainchi, Ma told me to drive on to the Vanprastha ashram on the other side of the Ganga because she wanted to spend some quiet time first. Arriving there, I went to the office to request for suitable accommodation.

Before I could even say anything, the manager informed me that the entire ashram had been booked by Sri Sri Ravishankar's trust. It was late noon by now, and Ma and the accompanying Mai-s were tired. I requested the manager to provide an apartment just for the night, thinking that this would give me time to find an alternate accommodation. He was kind enough to give me the key to a set of rooms facing the river.

Within an hour, we had all settled down. Ma called me and said, 'Yahaan kitna achcha hai. Ganga ji ke darshan ho rahen hain. Hum yahan nahi rah sakte?' (It is so nice here. We have Ganga ji's darshan all the time. Can we not stay here?) I told Ma that the accommodation was booked out for someone else, but tomorrow we will find an even better place to stay. After an hour or so, Ma called me again, 'Hum yahaan rah sakte to kitna achcha hota.' (If we could have stayed here, it would have been so nice.) I was used to this; Ma was such a sweet and persuasive child at times. I knelt down by her bed, and stroking her hand gently, I explained the situation. However, there was so much remorse in my heart for not being able to do anything in this matter.

The next morning, I resolved to go looking for a suitable place when the manager sent for me. In the reception area, I saw a gentleman seated on the sofa, quite distinctive in his colourful shorts. Thinking that the manager had called me to ask when we were leaving, even before he spoke, I said we would vacate the rooms in a couple of hours. The gentleman on the sofa spoke up now. 'Behen,' he said, 'Those rooms were booked in my name, for some of my relatives. I hear that there are elderly ladies with you. It appears that my relatives have cancelled their plans, so I would request you to stay on.'

Unbelievable as it all sounded, I quickly took out the money to pay for the rooms for an extended stay. The gentleman said, 'I just called you "Behen". I cannot accept money from my sister.' Later, I got to know his name was Mr Dholakia.

One evening, seeing the mothers walking by, he came and asked me, 'Who are they? They look so deeply satvik, so serene and calm. Can I meet them sometime?'

On the day of our departure, I remembered the promise made to Dholakia ji to get him an audience with Ma. I went looking for him and found out that he had taken a vow of silence in a meditation camp. I told him that Ma would be leaving soon. For a second, I saw a look of indecision on his face. Then he said, 'Silence is for the samsara, for this world. I will come to meet the Devi. This maun is not for her.' Ma gave him the most beautiful darshan.

*

When in Rishikesh, occasionally, Ma would express her wish to be driven to Har Ki Pauri in Haridwar, which is the most sacred point on the bank of the Ganga river for Ganga snaan.

The ladies in the ashram would go with her. This was a day we all looked forward to very much. A dip in the Ganga, and that too with Ma, was a rare privilege. After bathing and making a simple offering of flowers and milk, Ma would, in a deep and sonorous voice, sing the arati 'Namo Gange tarange paap haari, sada jai ho sada jai ho tumhari . . .' with us. Subhash Arora ji, a senior devotee from Rishikesh, who escorted us on these trips, would invariably bring jalebis and samosas, which we would eat after this, sitting on the steps of the ghat.

In our group, there were elders who invariably observed the traditional norms regarding the purity of food. When they would accompany Ma on pilgrimages, she would tell them to partake of food prasad in the temples and by the Ganga. Ma held that anything cooked on the banks of Ganga, with Ganga water, is pure. So, whenever we travelled to Allahabad or Haridwar, after every Ganga snaan, we would sit on the sand or the steps to the river and enjoy jalebis and samosas along with hot tea. Sometimes, even the mothers had a jalebi or two with us.

On one such day, Ma, Chhoti Mataji and a group of ladies were bathing in the Ganga at Har Ki Pauri. I remember that Mummy was there that day, and so were Devi Didi, Nandi Mai and Bina Didi. The time was around 10 a.m. It was amavasya[1] that day and the ghaat was crowded with pilgrims wanting to take a holy dip. We were almost neck deep in water, chanting

---

[1] Amavasya refers to the first night of the first quarter of the lunar month.

prayers to the mother goddess, when I saw a woman on the steps by the water.

She seemed about eighteen or twenty years of age, beautiful golden complexion, a vermilion dot on her forehead, gold ear studs and a prominent nose ring, but no covering on her body, apart from a folded yellow cloth over her head. Perhaps my mind was so immersed in the joy of bathing in the Ganga with Ma, that this did not strike me as odd that a woman could be standing amidst that crowd without any clothes. Instead, I put my hand out towards her and asked her to join our circle. She said, in a soft voice, 'Kya karoon, vastra nahin hain na.' (What to do, I have no clothes.) I replied, 'Toh kya, Ganga to sabki Ma hain.' (So what! Ganga is a mother to us all.) She took my hand, stepped into the water and joined us. Then, she held Ma's hands, and both she and Ma took a holy dip. In the meantime, I saw Chhoti Mataji fold her hands and say in almost a whisper, 'Aaha! Aaj to sakshaat darshan ho gaye' (Aaha! Today we have had live darshan.) It was then that it dawned on me that this was no other than Devi Ganga!

After the dip, she emerged from the waters. One step, two steps . . . and then she was not to be seen anymore.

Chapter 17

Visitors to the Kainchi ashram were aware that it was expected of everyone to first offer their pranaam to the deities in the temples before proceeding inside, either for darshan or the bhandara. However, in my case, it was either my impatience or my longing to see Ma that would lead me to park my car near the main gate, race across the bridge, through the courtyard, past the temples, straight to mother. The thought did cross my mind now and then that perhaps I was committing a sacrilege by not following the customary norm of going to the temples first. I thought I would ask Ma about this to remove my doubts.

That night, after taking prasad, both mothers retired to their kuti. Before they went to sleep, I would take two glasses of warm milk for them. Usually, the mothers spoke very little once they had retired, but today Ma asked me a few casual questions about my day at the ashram. I felt she was in a mood to talk and took the opportunity to put my question to her. I asked her if it was wrong on my part to not stop by the temples and offer pranaam before coming to her. Ma smiled and replied: 'Hanuman ji se pooch!' (Ask Hanuman ji!)

I did not say it out loud, but the thought that came to my mind was: Now where do I meet Hanuman ji?

Returning the glass to me, a smile still playing on her face, Ma said, 'Badrinath chalegi?' (Want to go to Badrinath?)

In a childlike way I replied, 'I would love to go if I could meet Hanuman ji there.'

Ma answered, 'Woh bhi mil jayenge!' (You can meet him also.) Saying this, Ma lay down and I sat by her takhat and massaged her feet till she fell asleep. I now went to the adjoining room to sit by the fire, that was smouldering in the metal saggar, to read for a while. The book was an old edition of *Vachanamrit*—Sri Ramkrishna's conversations with disciples—which belonged to Ma. It was very dear to Ma since she'd had it from when she still lived at home. As I turned the pages, an unusual picture of Hanuman ji fell out of the book. It was a rare print of a very dark-faced Hanuman ji seated in meditation. I had never seen one like it before and kept the photo with me.

The next day went in preparing for the journey to Badrinath. As was our usual practice, we set off from Kainchi early. Our first stop for the night was at Pipal koti which was about seven hours away. The morning after, we started for Badrinath around 8 a.m., in order to reach Joshimath by 9 a.m. As all travellers know, the one-way traffic 'gate' at Joshimath allows traffic to and from Badrinath at fixed times. As we gained altitude, I remember that the hill road was quite a challenge, and I was totally focussed on my driving. We had just crossed a slushy patch of the road, where there was a risk of the wheels getting stuck, at Vishnuprayag, when Ma called out from the back seat: 'Dekh dekh, pahaad ki choti par ek Bandar baitha hai.' (Look, look, a monkey is sitting on the mountain peak.)

I stopped the jeep and through the windscreen, I saw a peak so high that it was almost touching the blue skies. Way above, right on the top, was a monkey sitting cross-legged. The others in the jeep saw it too. I tried to signal to the rest of our group that was following us in another car by pointing my finger towards the peak. But somehow my message was not clear to them, and they did not stop. Anyway, without giving further thought to the unusual sight, I focussed on my driving again, as the road ahead was severely damaged, and members of the Border Security Force were helping cars to pass through.

We reached Badrinath around mid-morning. A busy day followed for all of us—making arrangements for Ma's stay at the Andhra dharamshala, accompanying the mothers to the temple for darshan, and organizing temple prasad for everyone's dinner. Meanwhile, the temple priests came to pay their respects to the mothers.

I remember we called it an early night as we all were very tired. Since it was the month of November, it was freezing cold outside. Sitting by Ma's bed, I was trying to warm her feet by rubbing them with my hands. She asked me suddenly, 'Hanuman ji mil gaye?' (Saw Hanuman ji?) I said, 'Where?' She replied, 'Kya kabhi koi bandar utni oonchi choti par padmasana me baith sakta hai? Voh itne door they. Humko itne bade dikh rahe they to vastav me kitne bade honge?' (Can any monkey sit on such a high peak and that too in padmasana? From such a distance he looked so big, how big must he be in reality?) I realized the truth of Mother's words. So focussed had I been on my driving that this thought had not struck me.

The child in me reared its head again.

I said to Ma that I had wanted to ask Hanuman ji a question, but he was so far away!

Ma replied easily, 'Kya hua? Phir mil jayenge.' (So what? He'll meet you again.)

In the wee hours of the next morning, Ma went to the Tapt Kund, the sulphur spring, for snaan, at 2 a.m., and after bathing in the kund, we went for the Abhishek puja in the temple. The latter half of the morning was spent in the sun, on the bank of the Alaknanda river. As if on an impulse, Ma got up and walked to the temple again. I followed her.

Unlike the pristine silence of dawn, it was a busy scene now with pilgrims crowding the area. After the darshan of Sri Badrinarayan, Ma went to the back of the temple where there was a large murti of Hanuman ji. Close by, there was a verandah where pilgrims usually sat and did their prayers, maybe conducted katha pravachans, and so on. I saw a sadhu sitting on the edge of that verandah. There was something different about him. I noticed that Ma had now covered her face with her dhoti, almost the way brides do in northern India. She went and sat on the floor close to the sadhu's feet. This was unusual too.

Intrigued, I tried to observe him even more closely. He seemed advanced in age, very tall and thin. He wore a cloth

Ma in Badrinath temple

around his waist, a similar one on the upper body, with a prominent sacred thread worn on his bare chest. His matted hair was tied in a knot above his head.

The sadhu started speaking to Ma. I could not follow what he was saying, except familiar phrases like 'turiya avastha'[1] and 'nirvikalpa samadhi'[2]. Mother was very attentive to his words. He then turned to me, and I now saw that his face was dark,

---

[1] According to Swami Sivananda, 'turiya' or the fourth state is one in which the individual soul rests in his own Sat-Chit-Ananda Svarupa or the highest Brahmic consciousness during Nirvikalpa Samadhi.

[2] That stage of samadhi when all ego and samskaras have been dissolved, and the individual soul is one with the divine.

and almost exactly the same as the photo of Hanuman ji that had fallen out of Ma's book. He started speaking to me, 'Jab ek ladki chhoti hoti hai to woh khilono se khelti hai. Jab badi ho jaati hai to uska vivaah ho jata hai. Ab uska pati hi sarvasva hota hai. Voh apna jeevan usko arpan kar deti hai. Ab usey khilono se khelne ki aavashyakta nahin hoti.' (When a girl is young, she plays with many toys. When she grows up, she is married. Now her husband is everything to her. She offers her life to him. She has no need for toys anymore.)

I got my answer.

Having found one's sadguru, there is no need for anything else. All outward forms of worship fade away.

At this point, Ma's presence started being noticed by the pilgrims at the temple. Ma got up and offered a quick pranaam to the sadhu and started to walk away. I ran to catch up with her. She asked me if I had given anything to the sadhu. I said I hadn't but there was money in my pocket. Ma told me to go immediately and offer it to him. I rushed back. All this happened in less than a minute, within a distance of not more than fifty yards. When I reached the spot, there was no one there. I searched the temple inside and out, I looked in the small market, and in all possible places where the sadhus usually sat, but he was gone.

Chapter 18

My fondest memory of Badrinath is one of driving into the valley, with the Nara and Narayan mountains on either side covered in snow. The usual time for Ma's visit to Badrinath was in the month of October or early November, after the Navratri puja in Kainchi, and it would often coincide with the festival of Deepavali. With only a few days left for the closure of the temple, there would hardly be any pilgrims left in Badrinath. The small market, which was the main hub of activity, now looked deserted. Most of the shops were locked and covered with planks and tin sheets to protect them from snow. However, a number of mysterious-looking ascetics could be seen seated in clusters—long-haired, wearing tattered rags, smoking cannabis with chillums in their hands.

In Badrinath, we always stayed at the Andhra Dharamshala. Right below Ma's room was the kuti of Bhagwati Mai. One of the few saints who was contemporary to Ma, Bhagwati Mai was of Nepalese origin, and having been widowed at the early age of sixteen, she had come to Badrinath on a pilgrimage with her

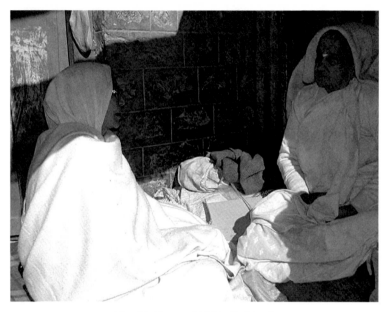

Ma with Bhagwati Mai in Badrinath

parents. Upon reaching the temple, after a journey undertaken largely on foot, she had a divine revelation, and she resolved to spend her entire life at the feet of the Lord of Badri, Sri Badrinarayan.

In Badrinath, every morning when the temple doors opened, as early as 4 a.m., Bhagwati Mai would be the first one to walk up the steps to the mandir. Chanting Sanskrit slokas from the Srimad Bhagvat in her beautiful sonorous voice, she would circumambulate the temple. On ekadashi (the eleventh day of every lunar fortnight of the Hindu calendar), Bhagwati Mai would sit in padmasana on the Narada Shila, on the Alaknanda river, and recite the entire Srimad Bhagwat Purana

157

from dawn to dusk, undeterred by rain, hail or snow. She could recite the 88,000 slokas of the Srimad Bhagvat from memory.

Invariably, when we reached Badrinath, temperatures would be down to sub-zero. While we got busy settling the mothers in, Ma's first welcome came from Bhagwati Mai, in the form of a burning wood fire in a metal container, followed by hot potatoes cooked in mustard oil and tea. Nothing could be more desirable in that weather!

In that freezing cold of Badrinath, Ma always went to the Tapta Kund for a holy dip, any time between midnight and 2 a.m. I learnt that Maharaj ji had told the mothers that whenever they were in Badrinath, they should be the first ones to bathe in the sulphur springs. And so, Ma and Chhoti Mataji barely slept at night. As soon as the moment was right, Ma would walk out of the dharamshala, bare feet in ankle-deep snow, Chhoti Mataji following her. And behind them, one or two of us, holding a basket with their clothes.

We walked down the steps leading to the kund in the darkness of that cold night that was broken only by dim bulbs strung on poles that cast little pools of light on our way. Clouds of steam would be gushing out of the sulphur water in the Tapta Kund. According to the legend, Agni Dev had once asked Badrinath ji how he could serve him. Badrinath ji had said that Agni should flow in the form of water for the pilgrims who came for Badrinath ji's darshan. And so, the god of fire took the form of the sulphur water in the Tapta Kund.

Oblivious to the very high temperatures of the water, Ma would step into the Kund. The rest of us found it very difficult to keep up with her effortless pace. Ma would go as close as possible to the source of the hot water and recite some mantras and Hanuman Chalisa. We knew that sulphur fumes could be toxic and most ordinary people would be out of the Kund in less than a minute.

I remember, however, that we had some of the most exquisite darshans of sages during these snaans.

It was the night of Sharad Purnima one year. As Ma entered the Kund, a sage with lotus-like eyes was sitting in padmasana at the edge of the water, near the Gaumukh. Seeing Ma, he said, 'Tum aa gaye. Aaj Sharad Purnima hai. Paani bahut garam hai, lo mere kamandalu[1] se naha lo.' (You have come. It's Sharad Purnima today. The water's very hot, use my kamandalu to take your bath.) After saying these words, he walked a few steps, and was not seen thereafter. Later, Ma left his kamandalu by the kund.

On another occasion, another year, an old sadhu with jataas so long that they were nearly sweeping the ground, was crouching in a corner and singing stutis in praise of Sri Radha. After Ma had taken her snaan, she was standing in the fuming hot water, reciting prayers. I was next to her. I saw the sadhu dive into the Kund, swim to Ma underwater and touch her feet. Then he came out and slowly walked away.

After snaan, Ma would put on fresh clothes, wrap a shawl around herself, and then walk up the steps to Badrinath ji's shrine. The temple would be closed at this time, and Ma would offer her pranaam at the doorstep. It would still be dark. One

---

[1] A pot made of metal or gourd, carried by sadhus.

day, after pranaam, she pointed to a light gleaming atop the Nara mountain. Ma said, 'Dekh, woh Kuber ka mandir hai.' (See, that's Kubera's Temple.) I looked up and saw an unusual glow on top of the mountain.

In my four decades with Ma, we went to Badrinath many times. But to me, it still feels like yesterday. I just have to close my eyes and I can see Ma on those dark nights, walking up to the Badrinath Temple. Her wet hair tied in a knot above her head, her form tall and stately. She treads on soft feet—almost in a trance-like state—a being from a higher world.

*

During one of our trips to Badrinath, a few members of our group expressed a wish to see Mana gaon, which is the last village and Indian checkpost on the Indo-China border. We drove to Bhim Pul, saw Mana gaon, and got a chance to talk to the beautiful women of that village who lived in the belief that they were the gopis of Lord Narayan. Then we spent some time in the vicinity of Bhim Pul, taking a short break, when Ma asked us if we would like to go and see the Vasudhara Fall. She went on to tell us that it's so holy that even a single drop of water from the fall is considered a blessing. A few of us immediately opted to trek there, perhaps more so because Ma herself wished to go. Some of us who chose to stay back took Chhoti Mataji back to Badrinath.

There was a narrow mountain path leading to the Vasudhara, and from here, it was a five- or six-kilometre trek up the hill. The dhara gushes down from a 400 feet high cliff, which stands at an altitude of 12000 feet above sea level. It was the month of November, and we had barely walked a few kilometres, when the entire scenery turned into a panorama of snow and ice. The only sign of life was red-billed choughs flying in the clear blue sky. These singular birds from the crow family have black bodies with red beaks, red legs and claws.

The trek felt never-ending.

After covering a considerable distance, we could finally see the Vasudhara—a thin silver stream, falling as though from the sky.

The last bit of the climb was extremely steep. After every turn on the winding path, we thought we were there, and yet, the truth was that we were still far away. Reaching the base of the mountain from where the water falls below, we saw a huge glacier—like a giant block of ice—almost forty feet long and not less than twenty feet wide. We somehow managed to climb to the top of it.

Looking below, upon the other side, we saw there was a steep drop down to a frozen stream, which separated us from Vasudhara. Unable to go any further, we simply stood around imbibing the celestial beauty of the scene around us. I then saw Ma taking off her sweater, saying that she would like to bathe in the Vasudhara. I was stunned. First, there was the steep drop from the glacier, a frozen stream to be crossed below, and finally an almost perpendicular cliff which had to be climbed to reach the fall. I said to Ma that it was impossible to go there.

Ma replied, 'Maharaj ji kahte thhey mai hamesha sath rahunga.' (Maharaj ji used to say I will always be with you.) At that moment, these words made no sense to me. Looking around for some sort of a path down the glacier, in that lifeless snow all around, I spotted far far away in the distance, a figure in flame-orange walking briskly towards us. I pointed him out to Ma, suggesting that we should ask the sadhu if there was any way to get to Vasudhara.

When the sadhu reached the top of the glacier, I saw that he seemed to be in his early twenties, and from the way he looked around, it appeared he was familiar with the mountain terrain. I approached him and asked if he could show us a way to the falls as Ma wished to bathe in the Vasudhara. In reply, he merely shrugged his shoulders. I did not know what to make of this.

He now took off his orange shawl, unwrapped the orange cloth around his waist, and with just a loincloth on his body, he started walking down the glacier. I noticed that when he had been coming towards us, his pace was fast, but now his every footstep was slow and carefully measured, his bare feet leaving a clear track on the snow. Ma started to follow him, placing her feet carefully on the sadhu's footprints.

We descended from the glacier and reached the frozen stream. The sadhu turned around, took Ma's hand and slowly walked her across the frozen rivulet. Next came the vertical cliff. The sadhu started climbing, holding on to rocks with his hand and propelling himself up with his feet. Ma followed him, and began to climb up with comparative ease. The rest of us formed a chain and climbed behind Ma, one behind the other.

Fear gripped me that if one boulder rolled down, we would all be in the frozen stream.

Finally, we made it up to the fall. The sadhu left us, and climbing further, he went to the highest rock at a distance, sat in a cross-legged posture, and closed his eyes to meditate. I was overwhelmed by the ethereal beauty, the grandeur of the fall. We all sprinkled a little water on ourselves. Ma suddenly asked me, 'Did you throw water on me?' Before I could answer, I turned around and actually saw the fall sway forward, like a curtain blown by the wind, to spray Ma with a shower of water.

I remember that it was a bright sunny day. The rays of the sun were falling on the water at such an angle, so as to create rainbows almost every second. And these rainbows, sometimes vertical, sometimes horizontal, would encircle Ma, as she bathed in the sacred waters of Vasudhara. It was perhaps the most beautiful scene I have ever seen in my life.

Later, we all bathed in the waterfall. As we had no prior plans to go to the Vasudhara, we were not carrying any change of clothes! Ma sat on one of the rocks, and we all chanted some prayers.

About half an hour must have passed when the sadhu, who was sitting high above us, came down and started to walk back. We too got up and followed him, almost frozen in our wet clothes. He led Ma down just the way he had brought her up. Once we reached the top of the glacier, he left us and went to where his clothes were.

His back was towards us. As he wrapped the length of orange cloth around his waist, I noticed that there were two or three big patches on his skin, upon his lower back. I quickly drew Ma's attention to this. Ma often told me that Baba had big patches of fungal infection on his back, from the days he did sadhana underwater in a lake in Babania, in Gujarat. Baba's vests kept in the relics shelf in Kainchi still have the mark of medicine applied by Ma on the fungal patches. Ma gave a knowing smile and repeated that he had promised he would always be with her.

The sadhu now started to walk back. Again, we tried to follow, but such was his pace that it was not possible for us to keep up with him. Soon, the orange figure was out of our sight.

On the way back stood the Vyaas gufa, the cave where the great sage Veda Vyaas is said to have written the epic Mahabharata. After sitting there for a little while, we returned to Badrinath.

This was the night of the Deepavali festival. Very few people could be seen around Badrinath. The scene was familiar: it was freezing cold; the lights were dim and the sulphur fumes from the Tapta Kund could be seen soaring high. Inside the temple premises, preparations were on for the special Laxmi puja which was performed on Deepawali night.

We offered our evening prayers in Ma's room in the Andhra Dharamshala. Jalebis had been ordered for prasad that night from one of the local shops. A priest from the temple came to call us for the Laxmi puja. Ma told everyone to go. A plate of jalebis was to be left behind, and the rest were to be offered at the temple. As I was about to leave, Ma asked me and another member of our group to stay back.

When all had left, Ma picked up the plate of jalebis and asked us to distribute it to the sadhus in the temple. She warned us not to be scared as some of them may react in unpleasant ways. We went out with the jalebis. It must have been about 8 p.m. but felt like midnight outside. True to Ma's words, some sadhus accepted the sweets, while some showed anger and refused them. As we crossed from one side of the temple to the other, we saw the same flame-orange figure coming towards us. He said, 'Main tumhare liye ruka tha.' (I had been waiting for you.) This was the first time he spoke. Taking the whole plate of jalebis from our hands, he almost ran down the steps to the Alaknanda bridge and merged into the darkness.

Chapter 19

The Kumbh Mela is one of the largest Hindu gatherings in India, held every twelve years, in four sacred sites: Prayagraj, formerly Allahabad, which stands at the Sangam of the Ganga, Yamuna and Saraswati rivers; Haridwar, on the banks of the Ganga; Nashik, by the Godavari; and Ujjain, by the Shipra river. According to Puranic lore, during the churning of the ocean by the Devas and the Asuras, drops of 'amrita'[1] fell upon these four holy places. And so, the belief is that, astrologically, at particular confluences of stars and planets, the waters turn into nectar again, making this the auspicious time for pilgrims to bathe in these rivers for spiritual awakening. The genesis of the Kumbh melas, held during these periods, may be traced to Adi Shankaracharya, who encouraged gatherings of learned sages at these spiritually charged places, to discourse upon and discuss the deep truths embedded in the Hindu scriptures.

---

[1]   Nectar conferring immortality.

The Kumbh Mela in Prayag is attended by millions of people, each one aspiring to a snaan in the sacred Sangam. The Kumbh of yore was, in many ways, very different from the Kumbh Mela today. It was a huge congregation of humanity of course, but a different rhythm prevailed, and it was certainly not as populated. Nor were there the kind of facilities as there are now.

In those days, 'kalpvaasis'[2] would leave their homes in villages near and far, and set up simple tents on the banks of the Ganga, leading an austere spiritual life, away from the pulls and pressures of the household in their daily existence. They would spend time learning from their gurus, hearing discourses, chanting the scriptures and observing vows, such as eating once a day and bathing in the Ganga. It was a traditional scene of deep piety, going back years and years.

Besides their meagre belongings, people from the villages even brought with them their domestic animals, and it would be a familiar sight to see a cow or a goat tied outside their dwellings. The small areas that the kalpvaasis had occupied would be demarcated by sowing barley on thin ridges of sand, and soon they would have a lush green boundary outside their tents. Cooking would be done in a corner in the open, on a wood fire, by improvising a stove with bricks or digging a small pit in the sand. There would be happy chatter, simple spiritual conversation, and sharing of food. Small children dressed as

---

[2] Kalpvaasi: a person who has chosen to live by the river for a period of time, performing austerities.

Radha and Krishna, with bells tied to their ankles, would dance around in the open sand. As one walked by, the sounds of kirtan with the rhythmic playing of cymbals, the Tulsi Ramayan, or the reading of the Srimad Bhagvat by a group elder could be heard all over.

In January 1989, Ma went to Allahabad for the Kumbh. Tents with basic facilities had been set up in the area allotted for Maharaj ji's camp, and a temporary kitchen for bhandara was organized, where khichdi and other food were prepared to feed all who came. At a distance, a separate camp was set up for Ma and the accompanying ladies. In Ma's camp, there were four tents. A small tin shed served as the kitchen.

On the moist sandy floors of Ma's tent, heaps of wheat straw were spread out and covered with coarse black blankets, which served as bedding for both mothers. (Straw is used in the villages to serve as mattresses in the harsh winter months of north India since it is an excellent insulator to protect from the cold.) In those cold nights, the mothers used two thick Gandhi ashram quilts, rather rough in texture, as covers. At the foot of their beds, I would roll out a similar bedding for myself. During the day, the blankets and pillows were packed away from sight, and we would spread black blankets on the straw for the mothers to sit and meet visitors.

An old black tin trunk was kept in the corner, covered with a red cloth, and this served as a puja table for Ma. Baba's blanket was placed on this reverentially. A little platform was made with ten or twelve bricks, in a small space in the centre, and every morning and evening we would light a fire with wood coals and dried cow dung cakes, kept in a metal container. This completed the 'decor' of Ma's tent. We would spend nearly two winter months here, in extreme cold, and the greatest luxuries of the world could not compare to its comfort and warmth.

At Brahma Mahurat, between 3:30 and 4:30 a.m. each day, Ma and Jivanti Ma would go for a bath in the river, accompanied by the rest of us. We would walk up to the closest bank of the Ganga. It would still be dark outside. The huge expanse of Mother Ganga shimmered in the moonlight. At that early hour of the morning, aged sadhus would be taking their holy dips. Their faint chanting of mantras would seep gently into the profound stillness of silence that reigned all around us. The chill, the dense fog through which nothing could be seen, and our bare feet numb on the wet sand: I can never forget those dawns. Ma, in her thin white cotton dhoti, always barefoot, walked on undeterred.

While the other ladies followed, Ma would invariably go ahead to quietly check the bank of the river. Sometimes, at night, the river would change its course, cutting away the sand on the bank, thus rendering it unsafe for bathing. Ma would also gauge the flow of water, and if the current was strong, she would remark, 'Aaj Ma bahut ugra hain.' (Today mother Ganga is in a fierce mood.) The water would be rushing forward at great speed. Ma would warn everyone with her to not take a dip that day. Instead, we would bathe with our 'lotas'. However, she herself would invariably walk a little distance ahead of the others, Jivanti Mataji alongside. Ma would first help Jivanti

Mataji with her bath, holding on to her hands carefully. Then, standing on the almost melting sand, she would bathe in the Ganga in the usual way, despite my best efforts to dissuade her. The ashram ladies respected this distance.

One such morning, after Ma had forbidden everyone else from taking a dip, she was about to enter the water herself. One of the Mai-s, in her eagerness to take a snaan with Ma, rushed ahead and jumped into the water. Within seconds, the wet river sand beneath Mai's feet got washed away, and I saw her drifting away with the current. Ma reacted in an instant. The distance between her and Mai must have been about three feet. Ma leaped forward, grabbed her arm, and began to pull her back. While doing so, Ma almost fell back on the sand, using her own weight against the strong flow of water. I managed to clutch onto Ma's back, to prevent her from getting drawn into the current. So hard was my hold that later I saw that there were purple bruise marks which my fingers had left on her back.

*

A few days after this, around mid-morning, Asharfilal, the watchman, came to Ma's tent and told me that there was an 'Angrez' at the gate hoping to meet her. It was such a cold day that I was in no mood to entertain visitors. Nevertheless, I went out to see who it was. There was a very tall gentleman waiting, who said he had come from Germany, and he gave me his card. He further said that he was a part owner of the Mercedes Benz company. Since cars were not allowed in the Kumbh area, he pointed to a bicycle, saying he had cycled all this way. He was very eager to meet Ma.

I carried this information to Ma and she asked him to be brought to her. As he was almost six feet tall, he had to double down to get into the tent through its small opening. Ma and Chhoti Ma were inside. The German saw the two mothers and observed the simplicity all around. Perhaps because he had seen the splendour in some akharas at the Kumbh, he seemed rather confused by the unostentatious surroundings. Ma asked him to sit down.

After expressing his gratitude to Ma for giving him an audience, he asked if she could guide him on his quest to meet some renowned saints in the Kumbh Mela. As usual, I interpreted the conversation between him and Ma.

Ma said, 'I do not know much, tell him he should have a darshan of Deoraha Baba.' I conveyed the needful.

Then Ma said to me, 'Ask him who his guru is.'

The gentleman replied that his guru was Nisargadatta Maharaj. Ma asked next what he had learned from his guru. By now, there was a look of disappointment on the man's face. In an arrogant way, he replied that his guru had taught him the state of 'shoonyata'.[3] He then turned to me, and pointing a finger at Ma, in a not-so-polite way, he said, 'Ask her if she knows the meaning of shoonyata.' Disliking his manner, I translated the question. Ma gently replied, 'Tell him I do not know anything.'

---

[3] The concept of voidness that constitutes ultimate reality.

At this point, the gentleman sneezed. Ma said to me that it appeared he had caught a chill, and that I should get him some hot Tulsi tea. I went to the kitchen, and it took me a few minutes to return with the chai. Instantly, I noticed a difference in the gentleman's bearings: his face was flushed, and he seemed to have softened considerably in that brief interlude. He took the clay cup from my hand and after a few sips, said, 'Please tell mother that what I have experienced just now has never happened to me before. I feel as though a lotus has unfolded in my heart. Tell mother that I would never want to leave her.' I conveyed this to Ma, and as was her wont, she said, 'No, no I do not know anything. It's a cold day. Drink your tea and then you must go now. You have a long way ahead.'

The gentleman finished his tea, took his leave of the mothers, and albeit reluctant to leave, he went out of the tent with backward steps, keeping his eyes on Ma as long as he could.

*

The planning for the pilgrimage to Kumbh had begun many months ago. I remember vividly those evenings, when, after the prayers, all the elderly ladies of the ashram would sit with Ma in the carpet room in Kainchi. In her gentle manner, Ma would guide the Mai-s on the minutiae of the trip. On one of these occasions, Mummy was present, and seeing her eagerness, Ma smiled and said, 'Mummy, aap bhi hamaare saath chalengi.'

(Mummy, you will also come with us.) Mummy was overjoyed to hear this.

Since in the winter months Mummy was usually in Shahjahanpur, Ma had asked her to join us directly in Allahabad for the Kumbh Mela. My second brother was driving her up. Somewhere near Lucknow, however, they took a short break, and unfortunately Mummy twisted her ankle there, sustaining a fracture. Naturally, they had to turn back. So, it came to be that on the day she was to join us, I received this telegram instead. Feeling the pain of Mummy's acute disappointment, I bore this news to the two mothers, who were then sitting in the tent. 'Mummy's not going to be able to come, Ma,' I said. Ma remained quiet for a few moments. 'Dekh kya hota hai', she said finally. (Let's see what happens.)

In my mind, that is where the matter ended.

By now, crowds in the Kumbh had started swelling and the festive snaans had begun. One morning Ma called me to her.

'Go bring Mummy here', Ma said.

My thoughts were instantly thrown in turmoil: I didn't know what to do. How am I going to bring Mummy here? And even if she arrives, how will she manage day-to-day with her leg in a cast? (In those days, plaster of Paris was used to make these casts, and they were extremely heavy. Mummy's cast would likely have weighed 2 kg!)

But as always, Ma's wish was my command.

The next day, I left the camp at dawn and drove to Shahjahanpur in my Gypsy. No one in the family knew I was coming. As I opened the door and entered Mummy's bedroom, I heard Mummy say to my second brother, who was holding her hand and sitting next to her, 'Mujhe kaise bhi Ma ke paas leke chalo.' (Take me to Ma somehow.)

And so we did.

Once Mummy reached the camp, she was *so* happy that whatever niggling worries I had, melted away.

*

On the day of the main Kumbh parva that year, the auspicious time for the holy bath was between 1 a.m. and 3 a.m. A message was sent by Ma to Maharaj ji's camp that all the devotees should bathe in the Ganga whenever possible during the day, as there would be multitudes attempting to take a dip at night. The group in Ma's camp waited eagerly for Ma's instructions. Almost all of them were advanced in years, but keen to bathe on that day. Ma pointed out to them the scores of people moving towards the Ganga, on the other side of the camp gate. It was a sea of heads, so close together that the ground beneath could not be seen! She told them it would not be easy to navigate this.

Ma put their minds at ease, saying that even a drop of Ganga jal was as good as a snaan. Asharfilal brought us some Ganga water, and everyone was happy when Ma sprinkled it on them. The day went on as usual.

After the evening prayers in Ma's tent, we took dinner prasad and retired for the night. Around 11 p.m., Ma woke me up, saying, 'Chal, Sangam chalte hain.' (Come, let's go to the Sangam.) Jivanti Mataji told me to get the clothes basket ready, and to go to each tent and tell everyone that Ma will be going to the Sangam in a few minutes.

Was I dreaming?

I couldn't believe my ears.

Excitedly, I went around our camp. When I woke the ladies up and told them Ma was going to Sangam, a few jumped up, others smiled and thought it was some sort of a joke, but eventually they all managed to get ready and follow Ma. Ma was already on her way out. I remember we made a long queue, holding onto each other's clothing, so we wouldn't get separated as we made our way through the thick crowds.

It was a memorable night. An ocean of pilgrims; spotlights beaming from towers; men in khakhi keeping vigil; announcements on the loudspeakers asking people to take a quick dip and move on. A spacious embankment had been created with sandbags to facilitate bathing. I had anticipated that Ma would, at some point, go to the Ganga, and I had prepared a bag with packets of milk, flowers, a marigold garland, coconut, kumkum and chandan. Reaching the Sangam, however, I realized that there would be no time for all this. It was going to be just a quick dip.

Leaving our clothes on a mat, Ma proceeded into the Ganga. Almost magically I saw the crowds parting before me when Ma stepped into the water. It was unbelievable! In that gathering of hundreds of thousands, there was no one within a radius of ten feet. Both mothers took the auspicious snaan, and then the others joined them. Ma held everyone's hand one by one as they took their dip. All the ladies, chanting prayers to Mother Ganga, formed a circle around Ma in the waist-deep water. Realizing this was my moment, I rifled through the bag. Opening the milk packets one by one, I handed them to the group. Then I passed on the flowers and the garland.

Instead of joining the circle around Ma, I entered the water and chose to watch from a distance. The moon shone brightly. Ma stood in the Ganga in her white dhoti with her hair knotted over her head. Her face glowed with an unusual radiance. Milk was streaming down her form, the flower petals sailed along, and finally, the orange marigold garland was placed around her neck. The waters around her glinted in the moonlight. To me, the divine beauty of this scene was akin to the most beautiful poetic renderings of Sri Krishna's raas leela with the gopis.

I remained afar. Then I saw Ma's eyes searching around for something. When her eyes alighted on me, she swiftly took the garland off her neck and flung it to me saying, 'Sevak ka sthaan sabse ooncha.' (The one who serves a revered person holds the highest place.) Ma called me to her. Holding her hand, I took my holy dip.

*

On our way back, we waded through the thick crowds, protecting both mothers by forming a cordon around them. It was 2 a.m. when we reached the camp. The only person who was not able to accompany Ma that night was mummy because her leg was in a cast.

I had barely settled the mothers in the tent when Ma said to me, 'Ja gari start kar, aur Mummy ko snaan kara la.' (Go start the car, and take Mummy for a dip.)

I was dumbfounded to hear this. No vehicles had been allowed in the Kumbh area from three days prior to the snaan. There were spotlights with police towers all over, one of them, in fact, just outside our camp gate. How could I ever attempt to drive through that crowd? Ma continued, 'Jahan bhi Ganga paas mein ho vahan jana. Jaldi ja!' (Go wherever Ganga is the closest. Go quickly!) I called out to Nidhi and we wrapped Mummy's plastered leg with some waterproof plastic. Two other girls joined us. Everyone thought I had gone crazy because they had witnessed the scene outside.

Paying no heed to what anyone said, I started the jeep, we helped Mummy into it, and I asked Asharfilal to open the camp gates. Looking up through the windscreen, I saw that the guard on duty upon the tower was missing. It was incomprehensible. There was not a soul on the road, and complete silence all around. I remembered the miracle that had happened when Sri Vasudev was taking the newly born baby Krishna from the prison, and the gates had opened, the guards had fallen asleep, and the river Yamuna had parted to make way. Seeing Ma's leela, I drove out quickly and reached the banks of the Ganga. We helped Mummy with her snaan—she even had time to make her navratan offering to the river goddess. Within a few minutes, we were back in the jeep. I covered Mummy with a shawl.

As I was turning the vehicle around, it seemed as though the floodgates had been opened and crowds just surged in on the road from all sides. I managed to get us back to the camp in the nick of time. The guard on the tower was still not there.

Ma was waiting outside her tent, to see us safely back.

Chapter 20

I remember my first journey to Vrindavan with Ma in the mid 1980s. In those days, there was only one train from Kathgodam to Mathura. This was the Agra Fort Express, which was quite like a wooden carriage being pulled by a steam engine, emitting clouds of black smoke. It was an overnight journey, and as far as I remember, there were no air-conditioned coaches then in trains running on the narrow gauge. Being the month of September, it was unbearably hot. In that oppressive weather, sleep evaded us.

Sometime in the middle of the night, the train pulled into the Kasganj station, which was well known to the passengers on the train for the special tea in clay cups that were sold by the vendors at the railway platform. About twenty of us travelling with Ma would be up for that cup of tea. It was almost the highlight of the journey! We would carry tea in kulhars for the mothers, to their cabin, and they seemed to enjoy it too. (Two of these clay cups from which the mothers drank tea in Kasganj were saved by me one year and are now preserved in the archives.)

The train reached Mathura at an unearthly hour in the morning, never at the scheduled time, and there would be no porters on the platform to help with our baggage, of which there was plenty. Once outside the railway station, the few available taxis were old and battered Ambassador cars, which had to be given a push by the men to get the ignition started. Then came the rattling ride for the next fourteen kilometres to Vrindavan.

Reaching the ashram, I saw that Maharaj ji's kuti had been kept as it was, and Ma went in there first to offer her pranaam. Maharaj ji would spend most of the time on the verandah outside, where his takhat had been preserved. On the other side of the verandah was the kuti in which Ma stayed. It was comparatively small in size. One window and a shelf on the wall, which served as an altar for Maharaj ji's blanket, and that was all. Even after the long and tiring journey in that weather, the mothers seemed very comfortable and happy, having never even desired for anything more than what was there.

The mothers' room opened to a little passage with another very small room, which served as a store for essentials and also for keeping heaps of fruit and boxes of laddus, which Ma liked to give out as prasad. It was all very organized, kept scrupulously neat and clean.

In the passage, by the inner door to Maharaj ji's kuti from the other side, was kept a rectangular piece of wood. Ma would tell me that she often used this as a pillow at night and then, in a humorous way, she would say that in daytime, it was her almirah. Paying attention, I saw that carefully kept on it were their small essentials: combs, hair oil, soap. I could also see a match box and a candle, as electrical failures were frequent in Vrindavan.

Anant Chaturdashi, which was the day Maharaj ji took mahasamadhi, would invariably fall in September, and the mothers would be in Vrindavan on that day. Although prayers and prasad would be offered in all of Maharaj ji's temples on Anant Chaturdashi, the main bhandara would be held in the Vrindavan ashram—since Maharaj ji had chosen this sacred bhoomi for his mahaprayan, and a temple now stood where his last rites had been performed.

Thousands of devotees would pay their homage to him on this day, and they came from places far—as far as the US— and near; from Neem Karoli, from Akbarpur and Ujhani, from Hathras and Agra. The entire ashram would be full of people and crowds would line up outside the darshan room. Observing a fast from the morning of Ananata Chaturdashi till the next day, and subsisting only on sips of lemon water, Ma would meet every single devotee who came that day.

After spending a fortnight in Vrindavan, the mothers would return to Kainchi.

*

As is well known, Braj is famous for the celebration of Holi, the spirit of which lasts almost a whole month. The harsh winter would be over, and with the onset of spring, Vrindavan would be joyous with festivities, chants, and people singing and dancing for their beloved deities. On the way back from their winter pilgrimages, the mothers would spend the month of March in Vrindavan, before going back to the hills.

Before Holi, there would be day visits to Barsana and Nandgaon. Ma would go for the parikrama of Giriraj Govardhan. Visits would be made to Nidhi Van and Seva Kunj. The mothers would often talk of the days past, of being in Vrindavan with Maharaj ji. Before the ashram came up, they used to stay in a dharamshala in Gopeshwar. After Maharaj ji's seva, they would go and see raas leelas, which would be enacted all over Vrindavan in the month of shravan. Talking of these times, Ma would often mention Ma Anandamayi, Haridas Baba and other sages.

Soon it was time for Holi.

As the legend goes, Sri Krishna and the cowherd boys of Nandgaon used to play with colours along with Sri Radha and the cowherd maidens of Barsana. It's at least a week-long celebration in Braj, and the scene in the Vrindavan ashram was particularly memorable during this time. Devotees would come and go through the day. Handfuls of gulal[1] floated in the air, tossed by all who came to Maharaj ji's temple. Many would offer a pinch of it at Ma's feet.

Ma chose to remain indoors in the asham through this time. The only exception would be one visit to the temple of Banke Bihari ji for darshan. Here too, she would go after dark. In Bihari ji's temple, during Holi, small boys, aged between five

---

[1] Coloured powders used on the occasion of Holi.

and seven, would playfully spray yellow coloured water on all who came to the sanctum sanctorum for darshan. The children had golden pichkaris[2], and the water had been coloured by palash flowers. It was customary in Vrindavan to go to Bihari ji's temple and be sprayed with colours—it was considered playing Holi with Bihari ji. The mothers, too, returned to the ashram, with bright sprays of pink and yellow colours all over their white dhotis.

In the small kuti, which came to be known as the darshan room, through that week, devotees thronged from far and wide, east and west. People queued up for a glimpse of Ma, drawn by her divinity, that was carefully veiled under the immediacy of her simple love and compassion.

Like Kainchi, here too there were varied scenes in the darshan room. A Baba would come regularly from the Gore Dau-ji Temple and bring bhog prasad for her on a leaf plate. Another sadhu would pluck tulsi leaves and bring them for the mother and he, in time, came to be called by us as Tulsi-wale Baba. Purushottam had a shop in town, where he sold canvas bags. He would walk in with one bag as a gift for Ma, and always carried two paans for Maharaj ji. An old woman, who, in earlier days brought rotis with a little pickle for Maharaj ji, continued to bring them for Ma as well. Ma would receive these with the greatest of love. In the middle of all this would enter a group of women—on their way to do a parikrama of Vrindavan—their pallus drawn over their beautiful faces, and

---

[2] Spray-guns.

they would sing for Ma the traditional rasiyas of Braj, folk songs describing the playful leelas of Sri Radha and Sri Krishna.

*

One of my most treasured accounts of Maharaj ji and the mothers is set in Vrindavan. Once, Jivanti Mataji and Ma were in Kainchi, when, one day, Maharaj ji suddenly left the ashram without leaving any message for them as to where he was going. Chhoti mataji was preparing his prasad in the kitchen above the temple, when Ma had walked out to the front verandah on some errand and realized that Maharaj ji was not on his takhat. As she glanced towards the gate, she saw Maharaj ji drive past in a jeep.

The mothers waited for him in Kainchi. It began to rain soon after, and there was a heavy downpour for over a week. The mothers eventually received a message that Maharaj ji had proceeded to Vrindavan. The river in Kainchi began to get flooded, the roads were damaged and all supplies to the ashram were cut off. There were only two or three people in the ashram at the time, one of them being Kunwar Das Baba. Seeing rapid devastation all around, Kunwar Das Baba requested the mothers to leave the ashram and proceed to Bhoomidhar, which is higher ground, as Kainchi was getting unsafe hour by hour.

The mothers decided to go to Vrindavan. Pratap, an old employee, arranged for a taxi and escorted the mothers to Kathgodam. A few kilometres before Kathgodam, all traffic came to a standstill as the road below the Sheetla Devi Mandir had been completely washed away. The only way to cross over was to wade through the water in the Gaula river. Leaving the taxi, the mothers walked down the hill. Pratap helped Chhoti Mataji, and Ma led the way across through the strong currents, in waist-deep water.

Having crossed the river, Ma's eyes fell on a Paarijaat tree laden with flowers. Forgetting the trials and tribulations of the journey, Ma began collecting the flowers in her wet dhoti, saying she will take them to Vrindavan for Maharaj ji. Chhoti Mataji, in her motherly way, dissuaded Ma from doing so, saying the flowers would not last till Vrindavan in the hot weather. As always, Ma listened to her. Together, they walked to Kathgodam and boarded the train to Mathura.

Reaching Vrindavan the next morning, as they neared the ashram, a small boy, with beautiful eyes and curly hair, came running to Ma and shouted, 'Lo phool!' (Take, flowers!) Saying this, he showered a heap of Paarijaat flowers on Ma. Chhoti Mataji recalled that Ma was covered with flowers that instant, and many gathered in the palla of her dhoti.

The mothers chose to enter the ashram from the side gate behind Maharaj ji's kuti. They knocked and Maharaj ji himself opened the door, exclaiming happily, 'Kaun mila, Kaun mila!' (Who did you meet!) Then, answering himself, he said, 'Thakur[3] aaye.' (Thakur came.) Ma would often reminisce that Maharaj ji's face had been flushed with joy. When she offered pranaam to him, the Paarijaat flowers in her pallu fell at his feet.

---

[3]   Thakur is another name for Lord Krishna. It means 'master'. In many Indian languages, it is now used to refer to any deity.

Chapter 21

Neem Karoli is a small village in the Farrukhabad district in the province of Uttar Pradesh. Unknown to the world, this little hamlet, remote and scantily populated, sprung into fame when Maharaj ji took on its name. It was in Neem Karoli that Baba lived in a cave under the ground and performed austerities for a prolonged period of time. Soon, his spiritual aura began to manifest and accounts of his mystical leelas spread far and wide.

There is an oft-quoted anecdote about Maharaj ji dating to these days. India was still under the British regime at the time, and when a British conductor asked Maharaj ji to leave a train compartment, the train refused to move without him. All the machinery was checked, and even though the wheels were turning, the train did not move till Maharaj ji was requested to board again. This and many other such enigmatic incidents led people to throng at the 'mathiya', the hut of Baba Lachman Das, who, in time, came to be known as Neem Karoli Baba.

Ma did not visit Neem Karoli village in Baba's lifetime. Desiring to go there, she once asked Maharaj ji to take her to

Neem Karoli. Maharaj replied that she would indeed go there one day. He said, 'When you go, thousands will come. They will dance, sing, and weep before you.'

In the years that followed, this is indeed how it came to be.

After Baba had taken mahasamadhi, Ma and Chhoti Mataji went to Neem Karoli and asked the people if they knew anything of the whereabouts of the cave in which he used to live. Almost three decades had passed since then, and no one seemed to have an answer for the two mothers. The elders in the village were of course aware of its existence, but they couldn't locate the exact place where the cave was. Over the years, the surrounding land had been repeatedly ploughed by tractors, and now there was harvest all around. The mothers went to the nearby fields the next morning, accompanied by a crowd of local people, all speculating on the location of the cave. A very old man walked up to Ma, and turning to the gathering, he said, 'Why are you looking here and there? Start digging at the spot where Mother's foot is.'

The men started digging and the mud hollowed in to reveal the existence of the cave. In spite of the passage of time and the ravages of nature, the fragrance of havan samagri[1] pervaded the air the moment an opening into the cave was made. A suitable entrance was carved out. It was like a mud tunnel with a clay partition dividing it into two chambers. The upper half

---

[1] Havan refers to a fire ritual performed on a special occasion. Samagri refers to the herbal ingredients of this oblation.

had pieces of coal and ash from the havan. Evidently, this was where Baba performed his spiritual practices.

Ma picked up some relics from there: two metal clasps which had perhaps been used to bolt a small door that separated the cave into two halves, two balls of clay which, in that part of Uttar Pradesh, were used to represent Gauri and Ganesh, and an iron tong with the words 'Baba Lachman Das' engraved on it. She even picked up the pieces of coal scattered around, and the vibhuti or sacred ash that was found in the cave.

Around that time, an old man in the village, unable to walk because of age, asked to be carried to Ma. When he came to her, he narrated that, before leaving Neem Karoli, Maharaj ji had given him an iron tong, asking him to keep it safe, and to give it back to him when he returned. Maharaj ji did not come to Neem Karoli after that, and he took mahasamadhi in 1973. The old man then narrated to Ma that Maharaj ji had come in his dream and told him that Ma was in Neem Karoli, and that he should give the tongs to her. The mothers brought all these relics back with them to Kainchi and they are safely kept in Maharaj ji's kuti.

*

As we have seen, Ma's travel plans were almost always spontaneous. Naturally, there could be no planning in advance, and most certainly, no prior announcement of her visits was neither possible nor allowed by Ma. As there were no cell phones and telephones in Neem Karoli then, it completely

Sri Ma in Neem Karoli temple

eluded us as to how the news of Ma's arrival had spread faster there than with any wireless system of today!

On reaching Neem Karoli, as we drove off the main road and the car entered the track leading to the Hanuman Temple, we crossed the village. There were mud huts with thatched roofs on either side. At the sight of Ma's car, the serene village scene seemed to liven up in an instant. Women doing household chores, men in the fields, children playing on the street: all rushed to the car to catch a glimpse of Mother passing by. The shouts 'Mataji aa gayin, Mataji aa gayin, Mataji ki Jai!' filled the air. The elders, who did not manage to get near the vehicle for Ma's darshan, were seen picking up dust from the imprint of the tyres on the muddy track and applying it to their foreheads. An atmosphere of festivity pervaded the village.

The temple courtyard would be full of devotees awaiting Ma's arrival. The people of Neem Karoli had a deep personal affinity for Ma. Their unembellished and forthright devotion to her made it clear to us that when we were here, Ma belonged to them, and any efforts to control the crowds would fall through, simply because Ma was theirs. 'This is not Kainchi', some of the villagers would tell us in a forthright manner, 'Here, Maiyya is ours.'

Much before sunrise, streams of men and women from villages all around would be seen crossing the fields and pouring into the temple. Women would come with their little babies wrapped in shawls and lay them down on the tattered floor matting on the verandah, in front of Hanuman ji. The entire courtyard and the surrounding rooftops would soon fill up. They would chant the Hanuman Chalisa till Ma made an appearance at the door, responding to the call of their hearts. This would go on throughout the day. Simple in their devotion, they would all rush forward on seeing her. 'Maiyya, Maiyya' burst forth from every lip. To be close to her, to be able to touch her feet, or even her dhoti, was all they wanted. Ma would stand in the open patio, visibly melted by their love.

On some days, Ma would leave the temple premises and walk out to the fields nearby. Neem Karoli being a productive agricultural zone, the landscape would be a vista of yellow flowering mustard fields or a huge expanse of green wheat. Ma would sit on the grass near one or the other field. Village women would come and crowd around her, and old ladies would hug and bless her as their daughter. Ma reciprocated in the same way and would happily allow them this proximity. Newborns would be thrown into her lap, and she would lovingly fondle them. Newlyweds would take the liberty of holding her hand and placing it on their heads as they sought her blessings. People with ailments would ask Ma for remedies.

Orthodox traditions still prevailed in the village that the daughters-in-law were not allowed to go outside their homes, except on festival days. The same went for the girls of Neem Karoli who had been married in other villages. They were allowed to visit their parents only on special occasions. But once Ma arrived in Neem Karoli, these constraints were waved aside. All the girls had the freedom to visit Ma. They would come to the temple early and get busy helping in the kitchen. Once this was over, the rejoicing began. Freed of their family duties, they would spend the whole day singing and dancing. They would even compose impromptu songs to express their love for the mothers! A long-time favourite was 'Mata ke aane se aaye bahar'[2] and 'Meri Kainchi-wali mata'.[3] So lost were they in their revelry that in the evening, Ma would have to send a message to tell them to go home before it got dark.

There is an observance that girls who have recently given birth do not visit the temple for a few days until the religious ceremonies associated with the child's birth are performed. So, girls with newborns would send messages to me to pray to Ma

---

[2] With the coming of the mother, comes the season of joy and abundance . . .
[3] My mother from Kainchi is here . . .

to give them darshan somehow. I would convey their prayers to Ma. Unknown to others, Ma would quietly go out of the temple premises, sit under a tree, and send for them. With tears in their eyes, they would come running and place their babies at Ma's feet. Ma would bless them. She would patiently listen to the hardships in their lives, console them, and guide them.

We, who accompanied Ma, could see how different she was here. It was a 'yes' to every wish and prayer made to her. In Neem Karoli, Ma was 'var dayini', the giver of boons.

The men in Neem Karoli kept a respectful distance from Ma, and got engaged in helping the temple management, as the crowd swelled in no time at all. They would bring buckets of milk from their homes as early as 2 a.m. and knock on the door of Ma's kuti, telling us that the milk was especially for the mothers. Each man with the milk bucket had the same message: 'Maiyya ko pila dena.' By dawn, there were eighteen to twenty buckets of milk lined up outside Ma's room. Ma would ask for kheer to be made, which was offered as prasad and then distributed to all who came that day.

As the day of Ma's departure came, the crowd would start gathering from the night before. The depth of their pain could be felt in their intermittent sobs as they sang the Chalisa for her.

When I think about Neem Karoli now, I remember most of all the couplet that would be recited at the end of the prayers every day by the entire gathering in the temple with great fervour:

Baba Baba sab kahen,
Maiyya kahen na koi,
Baba ke darbar me,
Maiyya kahe soi hoi.

[Everyone keeps calling Baba,
Ma, they do not call,
They know not that in Baba's court,
Ma's word is all.]

Chapter 22

A temple dedicated to Maharaj ji was established near the village of Veerapuram, at a distance of about 32 kilometres from the city of Chennai. With the efforts of devotees, a small ashram, with a kuti for Ma and Chhoti Mataji and a few rooms for the accompanying devotees, was built in 1984. A temple for Sri Dandayutpani Swami and the Navgraha already existed within the ashram premises, and a murti of Maharaj ji was consecrated in a small temple for Baba in the year 1986. Over the years, with annual visits made by the mothers, a Hanuman temple was built by devotees from Chennai, and then another one for Lord Ganesha.

From Veerapuram, it was also convenient for the mothers to visit the holy places of southern India: Rameshwaram, Kanyakumari, Madurai, Tirupati, Tiruvannamalai and Trivandrum. The Veerapuram ashram also provided a respite to the elderly devotees from the cold foggy winters of northern India. Along with the Mai-s and many other devotees, the mothers would spend a couple of months in the warm climate of Chennai almost every year.

The journey from Delhi to Chennai would be aboard the Tamil Nadu Express. The transition from the cold to the warm weather would take place as we went through Central India. The two mothers, sitting by the windows, would talk about the landmarks that dotted the sacred geography of the subcontinent. Crossing the ravines of the Chambal, for instance, Ma would point out trees with light-coloured trunks and tell us they were called Ram Kullu trees. It is said that Bhagvan Ram, during his exile from Ayodhya, rested under these trees. On other occasions, the mothers would ask us to take darshan of the holy river Narmada as the train went across the overbridge.

It was strange that whenever we reached the Itarsi station near Bhopal we would be met by some spiritual person or sadhu. This happened year after year. Once, just as the train drew into the platform, a sadhu with jatas and a prominent vaiashnav tilak came to Ma's window. Coming close, he recited the lines from the Ramayan, 'Tat mor ati punya bahuta, dekhyeu nain Ram kar doota.' (It is my auspicious good fortune to see the apostle of Ram with my eyes.) Another time, a baba dressed in rags but with a serene countenance stood by ma's window. After making enquiries about her welfare like a family elder, he blessed her and gave her two rupees before leaving. Once on a similar journey, as Ma went to take a wash, and I followed with fresh water and towels, there sat in the passage a beggarly old man with a very pleasant face. I stood next to him and casually asked if he knew who Ma was. He replied, 'Yeh to bhagwan hain.' (She is divine.) His face looked familiar and I sat down next to him.

After a few minutes, Ma came out to where we were. He reached out his hand to bless her and Ma bent down to receive his blessings. Then he put his hand into a cloth bag, took out warm puris and gave them to her. The puris were as fresh as the ones made in Kainchi each morning. Returning to the cabin, Ma sent Chhoti Mataji to meet him, and he blessed her with prasad in a similar way. Presently, the train drew into Itarsi station. The baba got up to alight. I went forward to help, but in the blink of an eye, he was gone.

*

Away from the hustle and bustle of city life, the Veerapuram ashram was like an oasis of peace and serenity. Our large group would be joined by devotees from Chennai, and it was like a big happy family had met after a while. Everyone would catch up with each other, the ladies would take over the kitchen, making prasad and feeding everyone, the men would conduct prayers and other activities in the temples, and the youngsters would keep the ashram clean.

It was a busy scene at Maharaj ji's temple with prayers, the Hanuman Chalisa being recited all day long and readings of the Ramayan. There was a CRPF camp close by, and after their morning drill, the soldiers would come and catch their breath a while. Pilgrims en route to Sabarimala would make overnight stops. Even the local villagers would drop in frequently since in the arid landscape, the ashram had become a resting place for all, and in the Kainchi tradition, there was always ample prasad for everyone.

For me, the day at Veerapuram would start with a morning walk with Ma. She would walk almost 4 to 5 kilometres a day in the vicinity, in the course of which she would, on some days, choose to walk through the Veerapuram village. On seeing her, men, women and children would instantly come running out, shouting 'Mathaji, Mathaji, Namaskaram!'

An old plastic chair would be put out for Ma. They spoke no Hindi and Ma did not speak any Tamil, but a very fulfilling monosyllabic conversation would ensue. Ma would be very appreciative of the rangoli—the artistic designs made at the doorstep of every hut with turmeric, vermilion and rice powder. She was also happy to see the well-looked-after cows, tied under the trees outside. Soon would appear two small steel glasses of 'palu', the word for milk in Tamil. Ma would gently refuse but ask me to drink it instead. At the end of it all, I would return to the ashram, over-nourished with milk.

On some days, walking in another direction, Ma's resting point on the way would be a dilapidated hut, arrayed with two wooden benches, in which, Mathai, an old man and caretaker of the small chapel nearby, ran a coffee stall for the peasants working in the fields. Mathai would greet mother with a loud and cheerful 'Good morning!' and Ma would wish him a good morning too. In English! While we sat there, Mathai would take out a carefully stored porcelain cup, perhaps the only one he had, and treat me to a strong, almost bitter, decoction of coffee and sugar. If, on some days, Ma would pass the hut without stopping, Mathai would get on his old cycle. He had an old bell on the bike, the kind topped with a metal bowl and a lever on the side, and clinking the bell energetically, he would try to catch up with us to greet Ma.

A small temple dedicated to the goddess Mariamman was at a distance of about 2 kilometres from the ashram. At dusk, both the mothers and all the elderly ladies in the Veerapuram ashram, including Mummy, would walk the temple. There was a big peepal tree with a well next to it. Evenings would often be spent sitting here with Ma. It was said that years ago, there had been a mound of mud and stones here, and the villagers respected this as the abode of the Devi.

Once, a British officer asked the local people to level this ground, but no one dared to do so. In anger, the British officer got onto the tractor to demolish the mound himself. The moment he neared the mud heap, the tractor was tossed into the air and overturned. The officer lost his life. Thereafter, the place was consecrated with a temple for Mariamman, goddess of the rain. Here also was a shrub-like tree, and its leaves were similar to the Indian ber tree. Ma would circumambulate the plant and bring back a few leaves with her. These were given by her to devotees for varied ailments.

*

Rameshwaram, one of the twelve Jyotirlingas and a very holy pilgrimage site for Hindus, was just an overnight journey by train from Chennai. Once again, it would be a large number of people travelling with the mothers. Arrangements for stay would be made at the Gujarat Bhavan.

The first morning in Rameshwaram would commence with a holy dip in the sea, and then snaan in the twenty-two kunds, or wells, inside the temple, signifying twenty-two teerthams. As the pilgrims went around, the priests stood by each well and drew water from them in small buckets and poured it on the devotees. The mothers led us round the kunds and the temple echoed with chants of 'Sri Ram Jai Ram Jai Jai Ram!' After the snaan, having changed our clothes, we would proceed for the darshan of Ramanathaswamy, perhaps the most sacred Shiv linga as it had been worshipped by Bhagwan Ram himself.

For us, it would usually be a three-day stay in Rameshwaram. On the second day, we would visit all places of spiritual significance, like Sakshi Hanuman, Ram Jharokha, Sita Kund, Laksman Kund and others. The third day would be spent in prayers in the temple and an evening visit to Vibhishan's mahal.

Whenever in Veerapuram, Ma would invariably go to Tirupati once. The Balaji Venkateswar Temple is one of the holiest Vaishnava shrines for Hindus, and once again, located at a very convenient distance from the ashram. It was about a four-hour journey by road.

After darshans at the Balaji Temple, Ma would visit the Japali Anjaneya Temple, about 7 kilometres away, also known as the Japali Teertham. From the main road, it entailed a trek down a rubble path to reach the temple. It is believed that Bhagwan Ram had stayed here with Sita ji and Lakshman ji, and according to the legend, Japali rishi did tapasya in the forests here, after which Hanuman ji appeared to him.

*

In the 1990s, Chenna Reddy, who was then the Governor of Tamil Nadu, was a frequent visitor to Veerapuram ashram. His devotion for the mothers dated back to the days when he was the Governor of Uttar Pradesh and would often visit the mothers in Kainchi. As news would come of his impending visit, the ashram would gradually fill up with security personnel. The Governor would arrive later, accompanied by his family members, and spent the entire evening with the mothers. Prasad was given to all of them naturally, but also to each member of his large security detail.

Amongst eminent visitors from the West who travelled to Veerapuram were Ram Dass, who had first come to Maharaj ji in 1967 and later became a renowned spiritual teacher in the West. Another was Dr Larry Brilliant, who had first come to Maharaj ji in the 1970s. He had been advised by Maharaj ji to join WHO as a medical officer, and later, as I have said before, he played a major role in the eradication of smallpox in India. Larry came to Veerapuram to meet Ma, accompanied by his daughter Sharda.

A very dear and honoured visitor to the Veerapuram ashram was Dr G Natchiar, the co-founder and director of the Aravind Eye Hospitals. Our stay in the South would always end with a visit to Madurai, where, under Dr Natchiar's care, we would all be given eye check-ups at the hospital.

The mothers' association with the Aravind Eye Hospital dates back to early 1980s, when Jivanti Mataji was operated on both her eyes, under the care of Dr G Venkataswamy and Dr Natchiar, who was his youngest sister. Dr V, as Dr Venkataswamy was called by everyone, was the great visionary ophthalmologist who had dedicated his life to the removal of needless blindness in India and founded the Aravind Eye Care System.

Jivanti Mataji had had very weak eyesight for a long time, and her vision was rapidly deteriorating. One day, on her return from Nainital after meeting the ophthalmologist, she was visibly depressed. Maharaj ji was seated on his takhat, and Chhoti Mataji was sitting nearby. She told him that the doctor had said that there was no cure for her eyes, and she would lose her eyesight at a later age. Maharaj leaned forward and playfully pulled her glasses off her face. Tossing them aside, he said, 'Jivanti lalli, tu door door dekhegi. Bombai dekhegi, Calcutta dekhegi!' (Jivanti lalli, you will see far-off places. You will see Bombay, you will see Calcutta!)

When Jivanti Ma's eyes were checked out by Dr Natchiar, she said that they could certainly perform surgery on Jivanti Ma's eyes, but there was no surety that her vision could be improved. Ma, remembering Maharaj ji's words, asked the doctors to operate on Chhoti Mataji's eyes. She was successfully operated upon, and her vision improved remarkably. When Dr V came to see Jivanti Ma, he smiled, and tossing her glasses aside, echoed Maharaj ji's words, 'Now you will see far-off places.'

During Ma's stay in Madurai, Dr V would drive his car himself when he came to take the mothers to the hospital. At the time, he was over seventy. I remember, one such day he took Ma to his office and requested her to sit on his chair. He asked me to tell Ma that he was working on a cataract eradication programme, and he would get good thoughts if Ma sat on his chair. In 2002, Ma was operated for cataract in the Aravind Eye Hospital, and once again I was touched to see the kind of care she received not only from Dr Natchiar and the attending surgeon, Dr Krishnadas Gandhi, but from every member of the staff in the hospital.

In 2017, Dr Natchiar brought a group of forty people, which included doctors and surgeons from the Hospital, as well as three generations of her family—her own children and grandchildren, to the ashram, to seek Ma's blessings. They spent three wonderful days with Ma, in Kainchi and Teertham, in the course of which Ma showered boundless love on them. Perhaps it was Ma's preordained goodbye to the Aravind family who had served her with such care through the years, for three months later Ma took mahasamadhi.

Chapter 23

The Jagannath mandir in Puri, in the state of Odisha, is one of the most important temples of the Hindus, dedicated to Lord Vishnu. Puri is also famous as a seat of the Gaudiya Math, and Sri Chaitanya Mahaprabhu, the supreme head of the Krishna consciousness movement in the sixteenth century, lived here for a long time.

Ma would make a pilgrimage to Jagannathji every few years. Sometimes, she would make a halt in Calcutta, where she would offer prayers at the temple in Kalighat, and journey out of the city to visit Dakshineshwar and the Belur Math. It would be, for us, a long journey of almost thirty hours by train to Puri. Since we were a big group travelling together, the entire bogie would be booked for us. The cabin at the far end would be set aside for the mothers, and in the berth above them the bag with Mahara ji's blanket would be placed. Even on those long journeys, Choti mataji offered her usual puja to the blanket in the morning and evenings. The raisins and sugar crystals offered by her as prasad would be distributed to all travelling with Ma.

In fact, whenever the mothers went on these distant pilgrimages to Puri or Rameshwaram, Dwarka or Pandharpur, a large group of devotees would accompany them. As described earlier, consecutive cabins would be booked for everyone. However, honouring the privacy of the mothers, a respectful distance was maintained by all. Yet, everyone looked forward to the unique joy of being together with Ma for these long hours. As far as possible, the Kainchi routine would be maintained: morning and evening prayers would be sung in the train. After this, we took turns to go and offer pranaams to Ma and sit with her for a few minutes.

Sometimes, Ma would call the elders to her cabin and it was then that some of us got to hear of the leelas of Maharaj ji. Ma told us that Maharaj ji liked to go to Puri in the winter months and one of the places he chose to stay in was the Doodhwali Dharamshala. In these conversations, she mentioned that there was a small Ram Mandir, close to the simha-dwaar of the main temple, and after taking darshan of Jagannathji, Maharaj would sit there with the sadhus. At times, he would join them in their kirtan, and, picking up cymbals lying there, he would play them deftly. His other favourite place in Puri, Ma told us, was on the sand by the sea. He would sit there for hours during the day, sometimes accompanied by devotees, sometimes by himself.

Both mothers would prepare his simple prasad, such as moong daal, lauki ki sabzi and a few rotis. They would wrap the rotis in a piece of cloth kept for this purpose and carry the prasad to the beach. On one such day, Maharaj ji got up and walked away, almost disappearing for a while. When he returned, in his hand was a white cloth bag. Giving it to Ma, Maharaj ji said, 'Le amma tere liye laya. Kal se issme roti lana.' (Take amma, I have got this for you. From tomorrow, bring my roti in it.) This bag is carefully preserved by Ma in the cabinet in Maharaj ji's kuti in Kainchi.

Ma's food prasad on the train would be mostly fruit, along with puffed 'Ramdaana' (amaranth), 'makhana' (lotus seeds) or 'panjeeri' (whole-wheat nutritional powder made with a little sugar and nuts) prepared by a few devotees. For the rest of us, there would be an abundance of food because everyone would have packed something or the other for the journey. It was like one big picnic—I used to call it Kainchi-on-wheels!

Despite having been on the train for almost thirty hours, on reaching Puri, many felt that this time had ended too soon.

*

In the earlier years, Ma would stay in the Bangaria Dharamshala, mainly because of its proximity to the temple. (In later years, she stayed in other places too, such as the circuit house or even the governor's house.) On reaching Jagannath Puri, from the moment Ma had the first darshan of the Neel Chakra, the metal wheel which is symbolic of the Sudarshana Chakra of Lord Vishnu, and the Dhwaja, the flag, on the temple-top, fluttering in the wind against the blue sky, there would be an evident change in her demeanour. It seemed that she had instantly merged into the divine energy of that holy place.

Both mothers and a few of us would walk to the temple several times in the day. Sitting in the temple courtyard, Ma would often tell us, 'Bhagwan ko dekho, bhakt ko bhi dekho.' (See the lord, but see his devotee too!) And it was true. We got to see some sights of exemplary devotion. Ma's favourite story was about Karmabai, a woman who was a great devotee of Lord Jagannath. One day she brought khichdi for the lord but the pandas (priests) did not allow her to offer it. However, the next morning, when they opened the doors to the sanctum sanctorum, they found grains of rice on Jagannath ji's lips.

Our usual day at the temple would begin with the Mangala Arati at dawn. Ma liked to spend the morning hours there. Her chosen place for darshan would be by the Garuda-stambha, where Chaitanya Mahaprabhu is known to have stood for hours, tears streaming down his face, eyes upon Lord Jagannath's shrine. The wall on which he rested his hand bears the impression of his palm. Ma would often stand here and place her own hand over the imprint. Right in front of her would be a view of Bhagwan Jagannath, his elder brother Balbhadra and sister Subhadra, who are also worshipped there with him.

Ma would partake of the prasad in the temple bhojanshala with the devotees. The food is served there by the Brahmins, on plantain leaves, and Ma would often say to us, 'Jagannath ji ka bhaat/jagat pasare haath.' (The rice-prasad of Lord Jagannath; the world yearns for it with outstretched hands.) After the first day, the pandas would carry the prasad in the earthen pots in which it was cooked to Ma at the Dharamshala. Ma had a particular fondness for the sweet jaggery rice made for Jagannath ji.

Each day would be a visit to one of the nearby temples, the Gundicha Mandir, for instance, which serves as a garden retreat for Lord Jagannath during the famous Ratha Yatra festival. Another day would be spent at the Chandan Talaab, where Lord Jagannath is taken on a cruise in festively decorated boats. We would also visit the Sakshi Gopal Temple and the Surya Mandir at Konark. Ma was very happy when she visited the Gaudiya Math for darshan of Chaitanya Mahaprabhu's paduka, and to enjoy the beautiful kirtan there. One day was reserved for samudra snaan (bathing in the sea), and everyone in our group—young and old alike—was caught up in the playful fervour.

Our favourite place, however, remained the Bedi Hanuman Temple by the sea. The murti of Hanuman ji is depicted bound in chains. The pandas at the temple tell the story that Hanuman ji had been sent as the watch-guard to protect Puri from being flooded by the sea. It is believed that once Varuna, the god of the sea, came to Puri, to pay homage to Jagannath ji and at that time, Puri was flooded with sea water. When Hanuman ji was asked how this happened, he confessed that he had gone to Ayodhya to have laddus, as in Odisha he was given only offerings of rice. Ma would always ensure that laddus were taken for Bedi Hanuman ji from Kainchi.

*

One day, the mothers took me to a nearby dharamshala where Maharaj ji had once stayed. Shlokas from the Bhagvad Gita were inscribed on marble on its walls. Ma told me that one night, while in Jagannathpuri, Maharaj ji appeared in Ma's dream and quoted the 7th shloka in the 7th chapter of the Bhagvad Gita: 'Mattah parataram nanyat kinchid asti dhananjaya/Mayi sarvam idam protam sutre mani-gana iva.'[1]

Ma did not find an opportune moment to tell Maharaj ji about the dream but the very next day, as he was walking down the stairs of the Dharamshala, he stopped by the marble plaque on which this shloka was inscribed. Tapping his finger on it, he looked at Ma.

Years after Ma had told me this story, I saw that in all the copies of the Bhagvad Gita in Ma's room, Ma had underlined the shloka with a red pen.

*

On one of our visits to Puri, we happened to be there on the Padma Besha day, when all three deities in the temple are attired with decorations made out of lotuses. There was a great surge of pilgrims seeking darshan that day. The panda came to our dharamshala and asked everyone to purchase tickets for darshan, as there would be big crowds. Almost everyone in the group rushed to the temple. Mummy, Mataji's sister Hema didi and I stayed on with Ma.

---

[1] 'There is nothing higher than Myself, O Arjun. Everything rests in me as beads strung on a thread.'

From the *Bhagavad Gita: The Song of God*, translated and with commentary by Swami Mukundananda, Westland 2021.

Nearing darshan time, we walked to the temple from the Bangaria Dharamshala. There wasn't an inch of space; it was packed with people sitting all over, waiting for the doors to open. Both mothers sat down right at the back, in a quiet corner. In that multitude, I observed a very old sadhu, who was struggling to make his way through the crowds, as though searching for someone. He stopped behind the mothers, looking relieved. At that exact moment the temple doors opened and the crowd rushed forward.

We remained at the back. As people surged ahead, and a little space opened up, we were able to move forward. After a few minutes as we neared the altar, eyes fixed on the shrine, I was startled to see the same old sadhu now come out of the sanctum sanctorum and walk towards Ma through the crowd. From where I stood, right behind them, I saw Chhoti Mataji fold her hands to him, and then she and the sadhu both turned to face the temple. Chhoti Mataji's hand was on the sadhu's shoulder, and the sadhu placed his hand on Ma's shoulder. The three of them stood like this in front of the temple for a while.

By now I had moved up close. After a few minutes, turning, Ma said to the sadhu, 'Isko bhi aashirvad do.' (Bless her too.) In that crowd, I managed to do pranaam somehow. Leaving us now, he merged into the crowd behind us. Then Ma said to me, 'Dekh ho gaye darshan. Kahin ticket kharidne se bhagwan ke darshan hote hai kya?' (See, we got darshan. Can bhagwan's darshan be had by buying tickets?)

*

While speaking of Puri, I would like to share a personal story here. As is well known, in traditional Hindu families, it is the custom to get a horoscope made as soon as a child is born. The correct time of birth is noted and based on this, the astrological chart is prepared by qualified astrologers, prophesying the good and the bad in the newborn's life. As a family, we were not ardent believers of charts and prophecies; so, over the years, three astrological scrolls lay neglected in my mother's cupboard.

One day, out of curiosity, I picked out the scroll that bore my name and unrolled it. With my meagre knowledge of Sanskrit, I could not decipher much, except for the last line, written in black ink with a bold reed pen. It read 'Alp aayu yoga' (prophecy of a short life), and further went on to say that I would not live beyond the age of forty-two. I showed it to mummy, who, with her implicit faith in God, firmly told me not to pay heed to it. Instead of putting the scroll back, I tossed it into my travel bag, to show it to Ma whenever I would meet her next. Soon, I forgot all about it.

Months later, when I was in Kainchi, I found the horoscope in my bag. I took it to Ma, more for the fun of it rather than anything else. She took the scroll from my hand, and without looking at it, threw it into an empty basket nearby and left the room. That was the end of horoscope for me.

About a year later, Ma made a pilgrimage to Puri. She was accompanied by a large number of devotees. The first few days were spent in visiting the temples. Once this was done, Ma sent the group to Konark. A few of us, including Mummy, stayed back with the mothers. Around mid-day, Ma wished to visit the Chandan Talaab. We accompanied her.

Reaching the pond, Ma walked down the steps and sprinkled some water on herself. I followed, took some water in my cupped hands and poured it on Ma's feet. And then, in a split-second, my foot slipped and I fell into the pond. I went underwater and the only thing I remember today is that something like the edge of a piece of wood hit my foot and propelled me upwards. When my head came out of the water, I saw two hands reach out and pull me back to the steps. Of the two hands, one was Ma's and the other was of a sadhu in ochre robes, who I had never seen before and would never see again. Ma held my hand and led me up the steps. Then, patting my back, she said, 'Jaa, alp aayu yog tal gaya.' (Now go, the prophecy of a short life has been warded off!) I was forty-two years of age.

*

The last and most memorable pilgrimage to Puri with Ma was in the year 2010. Chhoti Mataji had passed on in 2005, and Ma didn't travel much after that. Without Jivanti Mataji by her side, she had withdrawn from the world a little. And so, what made the trip extremely special for everyone, nearly thirty of us, was that it had happened after a gap of several years. Throughout the stay, Ma seemed open to everyone and everything, spending time at the temples, walking on the beach at dawn, sitting by the sea in the evenings and even appreciating

Ma in Jagannathpuri

the little things that the ladies had bought on their shopping sprees. It was a rare and joyous time. I now realize, in hindsight, that this trip had been a never-to-be-forgotten gift to all of us from Ma.

When in Puri, at sunrise, Ma would walk to the beach and offer pranaam to the sea, a deep look in her eyes. The waves would catch the golden rays of the sun, the water would be glinting, the rolling waves seemed to reach up to Ma. She would softly say, 'Ratnakar, Ratnakar, Ratnakar.'

Part III

Chapter 24

As I look back now at the life I spent with Ma and Chhoti Mataji, I can see how, from moment to moment, a little cosmos came into being around the mothers and me, which was complete in and of itself. The outside world, with its quotidian concerns, drew further and further away from me as I journeyed deeper into the

With Ma and Chhoti Mata ji

vistas that Ma's divine grace had opened up. Years passed. And one day, I felt I was no longer separate from the mothers.

By 2000–2001, time had begun to tell on Jivanti Mataji's health. Her strength began to decline slowly, and though simple things—travel, sitting for long hours—became difficult, she was still always there by Ma's side, come what may. And so, the focus of my seva shifted a little bit, as I began to feel that my need was more with her. I became a companion, holding her arm for support as she walked with Ma, feeding her with my own hands, and tending to her every small wish. In serving Chhoti Mataji with my heart and soul, the source of my strength and guidance was Ma.

One quiet evening in Kainchi, Ma and Chhoti Mata ji were sitting in their kuti. Lately Jivanti mataji had begun to sit meditatively, with her eyes closed. Ma looked at her and playfully said, 'What is this Jivanti, why are you always sitting with your eyes closed?' Chhoti Mataji also broke into a smile and replied, 'Maharaj ji ko dekh liya, tujhkon dekh liya. Aur kuch dekhne ko hai hi nahin.' (I have seen Maharaj ji. I have seen you. There is nothing else to see.) These words embodied the 'summum bonum' of her life.

In the month of October 2005, her physician, Dr Ajay Khanna recommended close medical care now for Jivanti Mataji. Since he was based in Dehradun, Ma decided that we should shift to Rishikesh. Chhoti Ma was very reluctant to leave Kainchi. Had it not been for Ma's gentle persuasion, it would have been hard to take her against her wishes.

Chhoti Mataji had to spend a fortnight in the hospital in Dehradun. Ma was by her side of course, and Meera didi and I were with them. I still remember that Jivanti Mataji was unable to sleep during those nights in the hospital, and in that semi awake state, she seemed to be on a different plane. She would constantly chant couplets from the *Ramcharitmanas* and sometimes say the most intuitive things.

One night, all of a sudden Ma asked me to make a call to Dr Anoop and tell him to stop driving. I was surprised. It was quite late, and so I hesitated, saying I would call him the next morning. Mataji insisted, saying that he is in some discomfort, and is stroking his chest. I dialled Anoop's number and asked, 'Are you driving?' He said he was. 'Are you rubbing your chest? Ma just told me.' He was very surprised. 'Yes', he confirmed, 'I am.' 'Tell Anoop', Ma said from her bed, 'He must hire a driver.'

After Chhoti Ma's health became stable, we returned to the ashram in Rishikesh. Even though she was physically still quite weak, she kept up with Ma every step of the way, meeting people in her wheelchair, reaching out to all devotees who had come, and saying a few words to each one. Now when I think of it, for her, perhaps her loving farewells had started.

Jivanti Ma's last day—20 December 2005—was like any other, except that she seemed unusually cheerful. She got up in the morning, and sitting on her bed, I heard her giggle like a child. I immediately turned to Meera didi, 'What did you say?' I asked her, 'to make Ma laugh?' Meera didi shook her head and said she hadn't spoken a word.

I noticed that even though it was daylight, Ma was still sleeping. That had never happened. Concerned, I woke her up. When she got up, she smiled and said that she had had a beautiful dream. 'Maine dekhaa ki tune mere aur Jivanti ki gale mein ek badi phoolon ki mala daali. Aur uss mala mein Bhagwanon ke gehne bandhe huye thhey.' (I saw that you placed a huge garland of flowers around Jivanti and me. On it were tied beautiful ornaments, the kind worn by the deities in the temples.) If I was intrigued by the dream, I didn't let on.

When I offered my morning pranaam to Chhoti Mataji as usual, she embraced me, and quoted a line from the Ramayana: 'khasi maal murat muskan . . .' I knew the context of course. When Sita ji goes to the temple to worship Gauri Devi, the garland around the goddess slips off—this was taken as the sign of Devi's blessings, and that her heart is filled with love for Sitaji. I did not relate to the significance of those words until Jivanti Mataji repeated them to me again in the evening, and Ma drew my attention, saying, 'Sun Jaya, Jivanti tujh ko aashirvaad de rahi hai.' (Listen Jaya, Jivanti is blessing you.)

We went on with our duties. The mothers met everyone who had come for darshan. That day, I remember, Jivanti Mataji called out to me more often, asking me to sit by her or stroke her hand. That day, we were to go to Dehradun in the evening for a short retreat. Chhoti Ma said to me several times, 'Ab chalo . . . chalte nahi ho? . . . Hum kab jayenge?' (Let's go . . . aren't we going? . . . When will we go?') She seemed so eager to leave.

We were soon packed and ready for Dehradun. Dr Khanna was to escort Ma's car, and arrived around 6 p.m. As he entered her room, Jivanti Mataji stood up to greet him in a very warm and affectionate way, perhaps expressing her deep appreciation for his services over the years. She went to wash her hands before offering pranaam to Maharaj ji's blanket, and then she walked down the steps to the car. She looked so happy; she was in such a hurry to leave.

Both mothers were comfortably seated in the car. I was checking the baggage at the back of the car when I heard Jivanti Mataji call out my name twice, in a strong voice. I got into the car from the back and came to sit between the two mothers. Jivanti Mataji held my hand, looked up at me, put her head on my shoulder. Saying 'Ram Ram' in a feeble voice, she peacefully merged into the highest.

*

In earlier years Maharaj ji would say to Jivanti Mataji, 'Jivanti lalli, jab tu jayegi, tujhe Ganga kinaare le jaunga, chandan ki lakri hogi . . . tere hazaaron ladke honge.' (Jivanti lalli, when you go, I will take you to the banks of the Ganga, there will be sandalwood and a thousand sons for you.) And so it happened. I looked out of the window in Ma's room and saw so many young men running around, making preparations for their much-loved Chhoti Mataji's last journey. Draped in red and gold, in a beautiful carriage decorated with red roses, to sonorous Vedic chants sung by pandits who accompanied the procession, Jivanti Mataji was cremated by the Ganga in Haridwar, on a pyre of sandalwood.

A part of Ma departed with her.

Sri Jivanti mataji

In 2006, on her punya tithi,[1] a Bhagwat saptaah[2] was organized in Rishikesh. After this concluded, we began work on building a temple in memory of Chhoti Ma.

Today, if you visit the Rishikesh ashram, you can spend a few quiet moments in this unique little temple that embodies the simplicity and serenity of Jivanti Mataji, who had served Maharaj and Ma with such love all her life. Inspired in design by a saint's kuti, the temple stands on a plain white marble plinth and is surrounded by marigolds and roses. Jivanti mataji's temple was appropriately named by Ma as Devapriya kunj, the garden of the one loved by the gods.

[1] Death anniversary.
[2] The reading of the Srimad Bhagawat Purana for one week.

Chapter 25

For Hindus, a touch of divine grace at the last moment before the breath leaves the body is the ultimate achievement of a life well lived. In my years with Ma, I came to witness a few occasions when Ma gave darshan to a close disciple before their journey beyond.

The person who had brought me to Ma was, in fact, my mother Kunwarani Premila Jyoti Prasada. She was not only my friend and confidante but also my first spiritual preceptor. Mummy waved aside any constraints of the world that came in my way as she inspired me to a higher life, and then later, she too became a close disciple of Ma. She lived in the ashram for prolonged periods of time, and she accompanied Ma on pilgrimages—a constant companion on the ekaantvaas retreats. Even though she had been brought up in great luxury herself, she adjusted beautifully to the spiritual life of the ashram, maintaining her elegance till the last. To me, she represents the most gentle and exquisite blending of a disciple's soul with that of her guru.

After the sudden and untimely demise of my elder brother in 2001, Mummy suffered from a gradual loss of memory. I witnessed how she slowly withdrew from everything. Her greatest joy was proximity to Ma, and Ma kept her close, nurturing her with love and care.

It was the year 2002. Ma was emphatic that she did not wish to go far from Kainchi for her ekaantvaas this year, and that I should look for a place nearby. Accordingly, a cottage was found near Bhimtal, about 20 kilometres away, and after the June bhandara, Ma went there.

After we had spent a few weeks there, she called me in the morning and told me that I should call my second brother to come and stay with us for a day or two, as perhaps he has been

Mummy with Ma

222

getting anxious to see Mummy. Then, she went on to say that he should bring one of his sons with him. This was the most unusual, as our families did not know of Ma's retreats.

On receiving Ma's message, my brother and nephew arrived the next morning. They spent all their time sitting with Mummy, and she seemed very happy to be with them.

Two days later, on the morning of 16 July, Mummy went to do pranaam to Ma, as was her daily routine. Sometimes, Ma would also refer to her as 'Mummy'. Both mothers were sitting on the side of the bed, and they made space between them, asking Mummy to sit. This was strange. In Ma's presence, Mummy always sat on the mat or on a lower chair, but today she readily sat down between them. Then, holding her hand, I heard Ma say to Mummy, 'Mummy aaj aapko jaana hai.' (Mummy, you have to go today.)

Smiling, Mummy replied, 'Haan Ma, aaj jaana hai.' (Yes Ma, I have to go today.)

The purport of those words was lost on me as, at that moment, there was a big flash of light in the room. We all saw it. Another lady in the room was doing puja and she almost screamed that a light had emanated from the small murti of Hanuman ji on Ma's puja table.

That evening, Mummy's blood pressure began to fluctuate. We propped her on the bed to facilitate easy breathing. Ma was told that Mummy's condition was not good. Around 8 p.m., Ma walked into Mummy's room, and taking her hand, she stood in front of her. My brother, my nephew and I were around her. A few minutes later, looking at Ma with a faint smile on her face, holding her hand in hers, Mummy passed away peacefully. It was the auspicious day of 'Haryali Sankrant', the wedding day of Lord Shiva and Goddess Parvati.

*

Mr Kehar Singh was a senior government officer who was drawn to Maharaj ji when he'd held the post of Commissioner in Lucknow. A recipient of Maharaj ji's immense grace, Kehar Singh ji was also blessed with exceptional insight into the divinity of Ma. For the last decade or more of his life, he lived in the ashram. The summer months were spent in Kainchi, and during the winters, Ma would make arrangements for his stay in Vrindavan. About eighty years of age, it was a familiar sight to see him walk around the temples in Kainchi for a glimpse of Ma. He never went inside the darshan room unless called by Ma. If Ma was sitting in darshan with many people, not wishing to disturb her, he would do pranaam at her doorstep and return to his room. This would be enough for him.

Since my room was next to his, I would often be called by him to carry his messages to Ma. Sometimes he had offerings for Ma, such as a dhoti or a warm shawl. He would go and buy these himself, and they were always the best khadi or the purest pashmina. One day, Kehar Singh ji called me. Incidentally, he had a strong temper, so it had become a habit for all of us to whisper a small prayer before entering his room. I saw that he looked particularly unhappy. His message to Ma was that he had not seen her for four days and he wanted me to tell her that he felt his time was near. I was told to come back and tell him what Ma said.

It was a busy day for Ma. Many people had come that day for her darshan. When she came to take prasad late in the afternoon, I conveyed Kehar Singh ji's message, and that he had wanted to hear her reply. Ma almost laughed and said, 'Aisa kah rahe thhey! Unse kah de, jab mai bhejungi tab jayenge. Aise nahi bhejungi, bahut shaan se bhejungi! Ja unhe bula la!' (Was he saying this! Tell him, he will go only when I send him. I will not send him like this. I will send him with great dignity and honour. Go call him!) Once he came into Ma's presence, he was his cheerful self again.

In the winter months, Ma left for Veerapuram in Chennai. Kehar Singh ji went to Vrindavan. Ma kept getting news that his health was not good, but it was also nothing serious. In early February, Ma and the large group of devotees with her boarded the Tamil Nadu Express for Delhi. It was a journey of thirty-six hours in the train, so it was a pattern every year to take a break for a day or two in Delhi before proceeding to Vrindavan. Many people were there at the Delhi railway station to receive Ma, each with a hope that Ma would grace their home and stay in their house as she did in the past years. We also looked forward to the break after the long train journey.

That year though, Ma got off the train, met everyone, and told them that she would be proceeding straight to Vrindavan. Many pleaded with Ma, some held her feet and begged that she should at least take lunch prasad before going further. But Ma was determined to leave right away. So the cars were lined up, and we all left.

Reaching Vrindavan ashram, Ma was told that Kehar Singh ji's condition was critical. After going to Maharaj ji's temple, she went to his room. He was confined to his bed, emaciated, but fully conscious. He folded his hands and responded to Ma's presence. Then Ma went to her kuti, and we got busy cleaning and unpacking as it had been a long journey. We slept early, but at 10 p.m., Ma woke me up and said she wanted to go and see Kehar Singh ji. I tried to dissuade her as it was cold outside, but Ma was on her way. On reaching the room, I saw he was gasping for breath. On seeing Ma, he asked to be lifted to a sitting posture. Ma sat on a chair by his bedside. Kehar Singh ji folded his hands and bent forward to put his head on Ma's knees. That is where he breathed his last.

Next morning, devotees gathered from all over. Ma gave instructions for continuous Ram-naam kirtan in the ashram. As the bier was brought out, it was heaped with offerings of flowers. Amidst the sound of bells and gongs, the blowing of conches, and the singing of kirtans, Kehar Singh ji was taken for his last journey, 'with great dignity and honour'.

*

Govindi Mai was an old Brahmin widow who used to come to Kainchi for Maharaj ji's darshan, and Maharaj ji would tell her to go inside to Ma. Completely untouched by the ways of the world, her purity and piety endeared her to both mothers. Being much older in age, Ma and Chhoti Ma were like daughters to her. She would address them by their names, calling out, 'Jivanti! Siddhi!'

Ma loved sitting with Govindi Mai and hearing her self-composed bhajans whenever she came. Every time, Ma would ask her, with a smile on her lips, where she had kept her money and gold ornaments before coming. Govindi Mai would come close and secretly whisper into Ma's ear that she had hidden it all in the coal drum.

When Ma came to know that Govindi Mai had not been well and had often expressed a desire to see her, she was eager to meet her. I was told that she lived in a place called Damua Dhung, but no one seemed to know her exact address. Once, while driving from Bareilly, we were about to go past Damua Dhung, when Ma mentioned Govindi Mai. I drove inside and parked the car. There was a row of houses, and we decided to go from door to door. It did not take us long to find Govindi Mai's house. Her two granddaughters met us and guided us to their house.

As Ma entered the living room, we saw that Govindi Mai was lying on a bed. Ma sat down on a chair, facing her. She was so overjoyed to see both mothers that she called out to her granddaughters in Pahaadi, 'Siddhi Jivanti ai rahin. Unaar lije doodh la!' (Siddhi, Jivanti have come. Bring milk for them!) Though Govindi Mai could barely talk, a beautiful conversation followed, and after spending a couple of hours, the mothers left after giving prasad to her. Soon after, we came to know Govindi Mai was no more. It was as though she had been waiting for Ma.

*

Smt Mini Narain's arrival in Kainchi did not need to be made known to Ma. As soon as she approached the darshan room, we could hear her call out, 'Jai ho, Jai ho, Bhagvati ki Jai ho! Ma aap hi sab kuch hain, aap saakshaat Jagdamba hain!' (Praise be to you! Praise be to you! Glory to the divine Goddess! Ma, you are everything, you are Jagdamba herself!) No matter how hard Ma tried to deter her, nothing could stop Mini ji from proclaiming the divinity of Ma. So strong was her devotion and such was Ma's grace on her that she rarely left Ma without having her prayers answered and her wishes fulfilled. The strength of her rock-like faith stands unparalleled.

In later years, Mini ji was diagnosed with cancer and was undergoing treatment at her residence in Ghaziabad. Before every chemotherapy session, her only wish was to hear Ma's voice—something that Ma made possible.

During this time, Ma was on her way to Chitrakoot. She was at the house of Mini ji's son, Sumant Narain, in Delhi. A large group of devotees from Nainital and Kainchi had arrived there, and they were to accompany her on this pilgrimage. The train reservations had been confirmed and all arrangements for the journey had been made. The evening before our departure, the whole group gathered at Sumant's house for Ma's darshan. Ma came, and after sitting for a few minutes, announced that she would not be going to Chitrakoot. Everyone was taken aback. Disappointment was writ large on every face. Then, calling Kamlesh Bhandari ji, who was present there, she told him to immediately organize a pilgrimage for everyone to Sri Nathdwara Temple in Rajasthan. To me, she said she would be returning to Kainchi the next day.

As we drove out of Delhi the next morning, Ma said she would like to go to Mini ji's house in Ghaziabad. The moment Ma arrived, the house, which hosts three generations devoted to Maharaj ji and Ma, was transported into a scene of joyous celebration. Boxes of sweets for prasad arrived within minutes. Mini ji and Prakash Narain ji worshipped Ma's feet with Ganga water, kumkum, sandalwood paste and flowers. Her lifelong wish being fulfilled, Mini ji did arati to Ma amidst the sound of bells and conches. The whole gathering joined her in singing 'Ma Jagat Janani Jai Jai . . .'

That was the last darshan for Mini ji. By 2012, the disease had progressed, and she was confined to her bed. Sumant called me one evening, asking me to please pray to Ma for her blessing as his mother perhaps did not have much time. I conveyed the message to Ma.

Ma said, 'Usko bolo Kainchi aa jaye.' (Tell him to come to Kainchi.) I did not know what to say! I repeated to Ma that Mini ji's condition was critical, but again, Ma asked me to tell Sumant to come. I gave the message, and Sumant arrived the next morning.

Ma was sitting in the sun outside my room. Sumant came there and offered pranaam. Ma asked about Mini ji and then she was silent for some time. Soon after, Ma extended both her feet towards Sumant. Taking this as Ma's message, I told Sumant to get Ganga water and wash Ma's feet. He did so and collected the charnamrit[1] in a jar. Ma then told him to leave as soon as possible.

Sumant arrived in Ghaziabad, and wasting no time, he gave the water to Mini ji. This charnamrit was the last thing she had. Then she said simply, 'Ma.'

This was her last word.

---

[1] Water collected from washing the feet.

Chapter 26

As I have said earlier, our search for an appropriate place for Ma's summer retreat in the hills would commence as early as April, so that we could select a house and have it ready by June. However, as the years went on, it became increasingly difficult to find a suitable place. By now it was the mid-2000s. Chhoti Mataji had left us—her absence creating a big void in all our lives—enhancing my responsibilities to Ma. The world around us had changed considerably too. Most accommodations that were suggested to us these days turned out to lack a pure environment, were noisy and polluted. In view of this, it was decided to acquire a piece of land and build a cottage for Ma not too far from the Kainchi Temple. Long journeys were now becoming difficult for Ma. Besides this, it would be convenient for her to move out of the ashram for rest, whenever needed.

Travelling all over the nearby Kumaon hills, we found a beautiful spot of land in Soni Binsar, close to Ranikhet, which is popularly called the queen of hills. As we arrived there, we heard the villagers chanting the Tulsi Ramayan in a rhythmic cadence. Adding to this auspicious beginning was the scenic beauty of the place and the cool mountain air. There was an old Shiva Temple on top of the hill, beautiful pine trees dotting the slopes, a lush green hillside where natural springs spouted out streams of fresh water: there was nothing left to desire.

We reached Kainchi late in the evening. I saw that Ma was busy with a large group of visitors who had come to the ashram seeking audience with her. It was only late at night, when Ma retired to her kuti, that I was able to tell her about our day in Soni Binsar, and that we had found the right place. She asked me more than once, 'Tu khush hai?' (Are you happy?) I said I was very happy.

It had been a cloudy day, but the weather had been calm. Now, all of a sudden, there was torrential rain, and high velocity wind with thunder and lightning. As I sat by Ma, the electricity went off. The temple bells began to clang. The doors and windows crashed open, and the splintering of glass panes could be heard. I quickly lit a candle. With me was little Gopal, a young boy who had been sent by his father to live in the ashram, and who was deeply attached to Ma. At that moment, softly finding his way in the dark, Gopal, nine years old then, walked in with a glass of milk for Ma. Gopal had accompanied me that day to Soni Binsar.

Ma sat up on her takhat. Taking the glass of milk in her hand, she asked Gopal if he had liked the place we had chosen for Ma's cottage.

Gopal replied, 'Ma bahut sundar jagah hai.' (Ma, it's a very beautiful place.)

The storm was still raging. It was pitch dark. Ma then asked him, 'Gopal bataa agar is vakhat raat mein tu, didi aur main vahaan hote, toh kaisa lagta?' (Gopal, if you, didi and I were there right now, how would you have felt?)

Gopal replied promptly, 'Ma, bahut dar lagtaa.' (Ma, it would be frightening.)

Ma turned to me and said, 'Forget this place. Make a cottage on the land given to you by your father in Nainital.'

This was the most unexpected turn of events after what had been, for me, an exhilarating day. The fatigue had barely worn out, when my thoughts started to rush in another direction.

*

Our ancestral house, Prasada Bhawan is also on this same estate, and so care had to be taken to ensure that Ma's residence would be exclusive to her. Now the process of building Ma's retreat started in right earnest, with measurements, paperwork, clearances, and so on.

I began to worry a little. It was already the month of April and we *had* to get Ma's retreat ready for her by Guru Purnima in July. To top it all, the weather forecast for that year had predicted early onset of monsoon for northern India. The land had previously been a peach and apricot orchard. Many of the trees had died over the years, leaving an unkempt mountain slope with rubble and bushes, and needed a lot of work before we could start building. In Nainital, the rains normally start in the middle of June and go on till September, accompanied by blinding fog. Declaring this an impossible time in which to build the cottage, architects came and went. There was much to make us sit with bent elbows, chins resting on our palms, sipping unnecessary cups of tea, if we were to get caught up in these possibilities.

However, we refused to be deterred.

Kamlesh Bhandari ji took upon himself the onerous task of constructing Ma's cottage in a period of few months, amidst adverse weather conditions. He came with a team of ninety- three men from Jaipur, who started work simultaneously. The land was demarcated, cleared, and levelled. With Ma's consent, Akshay Tritya, a very auspicious day in the Hindu almanac, signifying unending prosperity, was chosen for the 'Bhoomi Poojan'.

Ma was residing in the Bhoomiadhar Temple at the time. After much discussion and mustering up of courage, the group went up to Ma's kuti to request her to go to Nainital with us for the puja. They made an effort to assure her that it would be very simple and personal, with no outside interference whatsoever. As we have seen, Ma's way in Kainchi, Vrindavan and the other ashrams was that she would oversee the minutest of details before any formal puja took place. Once this was done though, she would withdraw from the scene. Rarely was she ever seen in the temple premises *during* these ceremonies and rituals. When she was requested to come to Nainital, she smiled, hesitated, as was her way, and then asked us to do the puja on her behalf. Since Ma was not going, the question of my going did not arise and I, too, gave the same answer. Disappointment was writ large on every face.

The pandits had arrived, and Ma made sure that all the requisites for the Bhoomi puja had been procured well in time. She had asked for the prasad to be prepared a day before, as the auspicious hour for the puja was at 4 a.m. the next morning. Ladoos were ordered. Puri, aloo, halwa and kheer were made in ample measures. Everyone was busy with the necessary preparations, but the joy was gone as Ma would not be there.

That night, midnight onwards, there was once again a huge storm. Again, the lights went off, the same banging of doors and crashing of panes, the high wind. Ma was awake for most part of the night. At 3 a.m., she sent a message that no one was to go to Nainital in this weather. The pandits asked for permission to go and do a short ritual at the propitious hour and return immediately. But Ma refused to relent, asking them to choose another favourable time during that day. All plans were stalled temporarily, and after consulting the charts, the pandits declared 12 noon as the next best time.

Early next morning, I got busy with my duties for Ma: her bath, her tea, her puja and her simple bal bhog of wheat porridge and milk.

Soon it was 11:30 a.m., and a message was sent to Ma that everyone would like to come to her for her blessings before leaving for Nainital. Ma came and sat in the outer room, and everyone was called. Everyone brought flowers. I am sure Ma was taken by surprise when all held up the baskets and showered rose petals and jasmines upon her. Kasturi kumkum tilak was offered at Ma's feet and I made her partake of a little sweet prasad.

Soon, it was time to go. Suddenly, Ma rose slowly from her chair and said in a childlike way, 'Main bhi chalti hoon. Nahin toh tum logon ko Kainchi lautne se pehle mere liye yahan aana padega.' (Let me come with you. Otherwise on your way back to Kainchi, you will have to come to Bhoomiadhar for me.) Then, taking my hand she said, 'Chal hum bhi chalte hain.' (Come, let us also go.) She went to the temple, and after offering pranaam to Hanuman ji and Maharaj ji, she got into the car. None of us could believe it!

Reaching Nainital, Ma walked to the construction site with such ease, as though she was completely familiar with the landscape and the happenings of the day. In accordance with the Vastu Shastra, three pits had been dug in the ground, in three different directions. Each was about 6 feet deep, and steps leading down had been improvised from old wooden cartons.

Ma performing Bhoomi poojan for Teertham at the foundation-laying ceremony

Though I tried to deter Ma from going into the main pit, she paid no heed to my words, and taking the pandit's hand, she descended to the bottom of the pit where the puja was going to be done. A chair was quickly found for her.

The mason was ready with the trowel and mortar. Ma placed the first stone, which was a piece of cement flooring from Maharaj ji's kuti in Vrindavan. Then, taking the trowel from the mason, Ma spread cement over it. I had taken pages of Ram-naam written by Mummy, and this too was placed over the cement by Ma. Then the priests started the ritual worship and Ma poured Ganga jal, and dust, water and flowers of twenty-seven teeraths. Ma had Maharaj ji's blanket brought down to her and the arati was performed.

Ma then bestowed upon the house the name 'Teertham'.

The location of Teertham is at 7000 feet above sea level, and naturally, it was very cold for the workers who had come from Rajasthan. Rainproof suits were provided to the men and the work went on amidst rain and hail. Having had their first darshan of Ma, a few workers pledged to not return home till 'Mataji's bhavan' was complete. Pages of Ram-naam from notebooks written by Mummy were plastered on the roofs and walls of what was going to be Ma's room, and Ganga water was mixed with cement and mortar.

*

With the tireless efforts and loving dedication of Kamlesh Bhandari ji, Teertham was ready in July 2011, and the eleventh was chosen as the date of Ma's homecoming, her 'Mangal Pravesh'. Now, a week before Ma's arrival, the house was sanctified. Eleven pandits commenced the recitation of the Srimad Bhagwat in the house. After this, the Ramayan was recited for three days in which everyone participated. Offerings were made to Naina Devi—the presiding deity of Nainital— and to the Gola devata, the legendary God of the Kumaon hills. A three-day bhandara was planned, and the gates were open to all who came. Cooks were hired from Agra, Jaipur and Shahjahanpur. Last, but perhaps not the least, artists were invited from Vrindavan for the performance of the Sri Krishna Leela. On their arrival, the chief organizer wanted to know if our guru ji would be attending their show. As per Ma's wishes, we had not told them about her, and since Ma never attended any functions, we informed them that the raas leela was only for the gathering. At this point, Ashok ji, the chief of the artistes, almost pleaded with us to organize a platform and put a chair at a distance, behind the audience. His words were, 'I have faith that Guru ji will come.'

The house was decorated with roses and marigolds. Amidst the Vedic chants, the blowing of conches, the singing of joyous devotional songs and the shower of petals, Ma drove into Teertham. The whole scene looked like a fond daughter's wedding. Maharaj ji's blanket came with Ma. After this was placed on the puja table, Ma entered the house. Arati was done. Everyone poured out all the love in their hearts. Some touched her feet, some held her hand, and others were overjoyed to hear her call them by their names.

As the day full of festivities came towards its end, the shamiana filled up with the audience and the raas leela began. After the famous peacock dance of the gopis, the character portraying Sri Krishna appeared on the stage. Almost simultaneously, Ma rose from her chair in the room. I remembered then what I had heard from Ma in the past: that during raas leela, the main performers manifest the divine forms of Lord Krishna and Sri Radha. Ma went out of the house and stood behind the chair that had been placed for her, right at the back, with folded hands. So engrossed was she in the divinity of leela being enacted, I had to persuade her to sit down on the chair. Ma watched the performance for two hours, and in the end, Sri Radha and Sri Krishna danced their way to her and played phoolon ki holi with Ma.

With this auspicious beginning, Teertham became a spiritual home for Ma. In a simple way, the routine of the ashram was maintained in the house. The morning prayers; bhog prasad thrice a day followed by arati; and the evening prayers, which were particularly beautiful. Ma sat in her chair in her room as we did the prarthna, sitting around her on the carpet. After this, it was time for dinner prasad.

At Teertham, perhaps the greatest privilege that came to me was cooking all of Ma's meals. To be honest, cooking had been an uphill task for me, but gradually I'd learnt to make Kumaoni food just the way Ma had eaten in her childhood. Just as Chhoti Mataji had, in her last few years, Ma too would ask me to feed her with my hands. For me, the best appreciation from Ma would be when, taking prasad, she would look at me and say, 'Aaj tu ne Ija ke hath ke prasad ki yaad diladi.' (Today you reminded me of food cooked by my mother.)

A day in Teertham: Ma spent most of her time sitting in the garden, writing Ram-naam in the sun. Sometimes, she asked me to read to her. The lilies and hydrangeas would be in full bloom, the birds would splash around in the bird bath, and langurs would swing from tree to tree. When Ma looked up, she would see the familiar mountain peaks of Nainital all around: Snow View, Cheena Peak, the Hill of Lariya Kata, Camel's Back. She reminisced, as she pointed these out to me, how in the past she used to walk in these woods for hours. As Ma sat in the garden in her beautiful silence, it gave me the greatest happiness to observe her from a distance, looking so happy, so at home.

Teertham

Once in a while, on a clear day, a few of us would organize a small cookout in the garden when all of us would participate in making the prasad, as Ma looked at us now and again, writing Ram Ram at her table and chair, which were placed under a shady tree. Receiving prasad from her hands, we would become children again.

Decades ago, I had left home for Ma.

Now Ma had come home with me, to Teertham.

Poojniya Siddhi Ma

Chapter 27

When the mother goddess comes in the form of a guru, she lifts you into her lap, and nurturing and protecting you, she carries you across the shores of samsara. This was the secret of my journey with Sri Siddhi Ma, my sadguru and my all. Swami Chidananda in his book *God as Mother*[1] writes:

> It would be presumptuous for us to think that through a few words we have understood even a little fringe of the garment which the Mother has thrown over Herself and through which she hides Herself. What we have known is unto the grain of mustard; what remains unknown of the Mother is like the vast shores of the oceans . . . our attempt at trying to speak about the Mother has not been in the form of an endeavour to know Her—if She reveals Herself, then only can we hope to know—it is an attempt

---

[1] Shivananda, Swami. *God As Mother*. The Divine Life Society, 1991, p. 109.

at a little flower offering, a little worship at the feet of the Divine Mother.

When I attempt to speak of the divinity of Ma in the following pages, I offer only a few glimpses that I had, over the years, while 'vast shores of oceans' remain unknown and unsaid.

MA AND ANANDAMAYI MA IN ALMORA

In the little town of Almora, Anandamayi Ma, the renowned spiritual saint of India, had a small ashram at Patal Devi. Her residence, as I remember now, was more like an old British cottage with an open verandah facing a cobbled courtyard and a fruit laden apricot tree. Ma Anandamayi would sit or recline on her takhat in the open and give darshan to all who came. It was here that our beloved Ma, as a child, would often go for darshan, with her mother.

One day, someone in the gathering was singing a bhajan of Meera Bai. Ma, a child of five years, began to dance. When the song was over, a delighted Anandamayi Ma got up from her asana and came down to Ma. She picked the little girl up, and holding her above for everyone present to see, she made the prophetic statement: 'Yeh to jagat ki ma hai!' (She is the mother of the universe!)

Many years later, Ma came to know that Ma Anandamayi was visiting Nainital. She went to meet her but was told that Ma Anandamayi was resting at the time, and it would not be possible to meet her. However, Ma left a message saying that she had come. The next day, Ma Anandamayi walked to where Ma lived. She waited on the street and had a message sent up to her house.

Ma had very fond memories of that day and liked to tell this story.

She said she ran downstairs to meet Ma Anadamayi. After expressing regret over not having been able to meet her the day before, Ma Anandamayi lovingly embraced her, and said, 'What have you got for me?' There was a toy shop adjacent to the stairs. Ma quickly picked up a toy monkey. Ma Anandamayi spread out her shawl with her hands and Ma placed the monkey in it. Looking at it, she said 'Arey! Yeh to tere isht Hanuman ji hain!' (Arey! This is your deity Hanuman ji!) In turn, Ananadamayi Ma gave Ma a ten rupee note as a token of blessing. The two mothers walked a little distance together and then, taking her leave, Ma returned home.

Many years later, I went to Almora for Ma Anandamayi's darshan. I was fortunate to get a personal audience with her. She asked me who my guru was. When I took Ma's name, she was overjoyed and spoke a few words in Bengali. I noticed that a toy monkey was carefully kept on her windowsill.

MA AND BHAGWATI MAI IN BADRINATH

One of the few saints who were contemporary to Ma, and who we have already met in the pages of this book, was Sri Bhagwati Mai. On one visit to Badrinath, the moment we drove into the valley, heavy snowfall started. Acting quickly, we helped both the mothers cross the bridge on the Alaknanda and proceed to the Andhra dharamshala. Meanwhile, by the time we unloaded the baggage and followed, the snow was knee-deep. On reaching the dharamshala, it was a relief to see both Ma and Chhoti Mataji sitting by the fire. We sat with them and warmed ourselves. After a few minutes, Ma asked me to go down and offer pranaam to Bhagwati Mai.

When I reached her kuti, Bhagwati Mai greeted me with the words, 'Narayan Narayan—Sri Hari, Sri Hari!' There was a little fire here also, and the small space she lived in was filled with smoke. I did pranaam and sat down. Then, in an effort to break the silence, I said something about the inclement weather. She replied, 'Beta, mere liye to koti surya chamak rahen hain, meri maa aayi hai.' (Child, for me a thousand suns are shining today. My mother has come.)

Again, a few moments of silence. Then, pointing to a hair on her arm, she said, 'Hum unke rom ke barabar bhi nahin hain. Voh itni mahaan hain. Ma toh sakshaat prem ka swaroop hain. Unko jaan paana bahut kathin hai . . . Aise sant ke bade bhagya se darshan hote hain.' (I cannot claim to be equal to even a small hair on her body. She is so great. She is the embodiment of love. It is not easy to know her . . . it is with great fortune that we get the darshan of a saint like her.)

The day Ma would leave Badrinath, Bhagwati Mai would walk with Ma across the bridge to see her off till the car. Often, she would herself carry baba's blanket bag and place it in the car. This was a rare sight for all those living in Badrinath, as everyone knew that Bhagwati Mai never left the Narayan mountain and would only go across the bridge when Bhagwan Badri was taken to Joshimath, and the temple was closed for the winter.

CHHAPPAN BHOG IN NAINITAL

The tradition of offering fifty-six varieties of food to Lord Krishna is narrated in the Srimad Bhagvat Purana. Sri Krishna lifted the Govardhan mountain on his finger to save the people of Gokul from the wrath of Indra, the god of rain. The legend goes on to say that Sri Krishna ate eight varieties of dishes every day. Since he did not eat anything for seven days, until the rains stopped, the Brijvasis (the people of Brij) offered him fifty-six kinds of food, the chhappan bhog.

Bishambar Babu, a devotee from Aligarh, used to bring chhappan bhog and offer it to Maharaj ji. One day, he arrived in Kainchi and Maharaj was sitting outside on his takhat. The moment he saw Bishambar Babu, Maharaj ji almost shouted, 'Yahan kya aaya hai? Mai Nainital main hai. Ja Mai ko bhog lagaa.' (Why have you come here? Mai lives in Nainital. Go offer the prasad to Mai.)

Maharaj ji's command came loud and clear. Bishambar Babu wrapped up his puja samagri and promptly proceeded to Nainital. It was unheard of that Ma had ever allowed any formal worship to her own self, but when she was told Maharaj ji had wished that the puja and offering be made to her, Ma quietly sat down for it.

In later years, I was a witness to Bishambar Babu's annual puja in Vrindavan. He would lay down various kinds of prasad, place a red and gold chunni over Ma's head, and keep the articles of Devi worship such as sindoor, bindi, bangles, red flowers, betel nut and leaves and alta (the red liquid paste used for decorating the feet of the goddess) in front of Ma. Then Bishambar Babu would sit in vajrasana with a bell in each hand. Ma too sat with her eyes closed, immersed in a deeply meditative state, with a radiant glow on her face. No matter how long the ceremony took, Ma would sit through it, and after arati, everything would almost immediately return to normal. Ma would again be her usual self, so simple, so human, almost shy to see the puja articles spread in front of her.

MEMORIES OF MUNNI DIDI

In the early days of her travels with Maharaj ji, Smt Munni Sah of Nainital often accompanied Ma. Ma would mention her while relating stories about these pilgrimages to the temples of Badrinath and Kedarnath. In later years, Munni didi, as she was fondly known in Kainchi, would occasionally visit Ma.

It was the month of November. A cold but bright and sunny day, when Ma was sitting in the open backyard, by the tulsi plant. A group of about fifteen or more people were sitting around her. After a gap of a few months, Munni didi walked in from the darshan rooms and came to where Ma was sitting. Normally, a person of few words, she said to me in a loud voice, 'Jaya, main tum ko aaj bataane aayi hoon ki Maharaj Ma ke liye kyaa kehte thhey.' (Jaya, I have come to tell what Maharaj used to said about Ma.) After she had offered pranaam to Ma, Ma asked her to sit on the folded black blanket with her. This was rather unusual as no one ever sat next to Ma. Then, Munni didi started relating experiences with Maharaj ji and Ma.

Once, on their way back from a pilgrimage in the hills, Maharaj ji and the accompanying group of people were staying in the Khurja dharamshala on the Triveni ghat in Rishikesh. Ma's husband, Sri Tularam ji, was also with them. She told us that one day Maharaj ji asked everyone to go for Ganga snaan. When they had all left, he locked himself in his room.

The river was in spate. The strong flow of water had corroded the sandy banks. Everyone got busy taking a dip in the Ganga. Suddenly, there were shouts from the people on the bank as they saw Tularam ji being washed away in the water. We had heard of this incident of course, and we had been told that Ma had jumped into the river and saved him. Munni didi said that she was standing next to Ma when this happened. She specified that Ma did not jump into the river, but in fact, she saw Ma walk on the water and pull Tularam ji back.

Once, Munni didi had travelled to Badrinath with Maharaj ji, Ma and other devotees. After darshan at the temple, she went to Maharaj ji and as she was going to bow down to him, he said, 'Ma ko pranaam kar, Ma ko pranaam kar, Ma jagat janani hain.' (Pay your respect to Ma, pay your respect to Ma, Ma is the goddess of the universe.)

After sitting a while with us that day, Munni didi took leave from Ma—taking prasad from her, she left, as though in a hurry.

Four days later, she passed away.

MA AND MAHARAJ JI AT VINDHYACHAL

Maharaj ji, accompanied by Ma, Jivanti Ma and a few other devotees would go to Allahabad almost every winter. As soon as his presence came to be known there, Allahabad became a spiritual centre for all. As with Maharaj ji everywhere, his doors were open to everyone and prasad was distributed all the time.

However, when there were too many visitors, Maharaj would leave for Chitrakoot, Varanasi or Amarkantak, the source of the holy river Narmada. Often, he would visit the shrine of Vindhyavasini in Mirzapur. On one such visit, Maharaj, along with the mothers and a group of devotees, went to Vindhyachal for darshan at Vindhyavasini Temple. A short distance before the shrine, a narrow path climbs upwards to the temple. At the start of the ascent was a small mithai shop. Maharaj ji sat down here while the group shopped for prasad and other puja articles. They returned to Maharaj ji, requesting him to proceed to the shrine. Maharaj ji took the puja thali from one of the devotees, and turning to Ma, he put the sindoor tilak and rice on her forehead. Thus, offering puja to her, he said, 'Meri Vindhyavasini toh Mai hai.' (My Vindhyavasini is Mai.) He then asked the others to proceed to the temple.

Years later, when we went to Vindhyachal, Jivanti Mataji showed me the sweet shop where Maharaj ji had sat and performed this puja to Ma.

THE EVENING OF 8 OCTOBER 2017

In the last few years of her life, Ma entered a deep transcendental state. She preferred to maintain a meditative silence, and I observed how her fingers were always tracing the name of Ram on any surface in front of her—be it the armrest of her chair, or the tabletop in front of her, or on the bedsheet while she was lying in bed. Ma was eighty-nine years old, still in good health, and had the most unique glow on her face. She continued giving darshan in Kainchi, Rishikesh and Teertham, though she no longer travelled long distances. But it was apparent to us that Ma had entered a much higher orbit now. Writing Ram-naam in her notebook is what gave her the greatest joy now, and sometimes we would have to gently ask her to take a break.

It was the evening of 8 October 2017, around 5:35 p.m. Ma and I had just finished having our tea, when the following conversation took place.

I had been reading a book on Sri Ramakrishna, in which it was mentioned that He had graced many of his devotees with a darshan of various deities like Goddess Kali, Sri Rama and others. As I read, a thought floated across my mind: would I also have a darshan of this kind?

'Ma, kya mujhe bhi kabhi darshan honge?' I asked. (Ma, will I ever get darshan?)

She replied, her voice clear and strong, 'Tujhko ho rahein hain darshan.' (You are getting darshan.)

Perplexed, I asked, 'Ma, kiske darshan?' (Ma, who's darshan?)

She tapped her chest with a single finger, gesturing to herself.

Stunned, I asked her, 'Ma, aap kaun hain?' (Ma, who are you?)

At that instant, her presence was more empowering than ever before. Looking directly into my eyes, she replied, 'Main Jagat Janani.' (I am Jagat Janani.)

On hearing these words, I couldn't hold my tears.

On the morning of 28 December 2017, at Teertham, Ma took mahasamadhi. The night before, she spoke to me for a length of time. She revealed many things to me and gave me assurances about my future, though at that moment, I did not realize she was outlining the path I was to follow in the years to come. Before she lay down on her bed, she called me to her and held me close. I saw that her eyes had filled up. I do not know what made me ask, 'Ma, aap mujhko chhodke toh nahin jaa rahe ho?' (Ma, you aren't leaving me, right?)

She replied, 'Kabhi nahin chhodungi.' (I will never leave you.)

'Ma, vaida?' I said softly. (Ma, promise?)

Her last word was 'Vaida.'

Promise.

Poojniya Sri Siddhi Ma's temple in Kainchi Dham

ॐ
नमस्ते देवदेवेशि नमस्ते हरपूजिते।
ब्रह्म विद्यास्वरूपायै तस्यै नित्यं नमोनमः॥
भवबन्धनवारस्य तारिणी जननी परा।
ज्ञानदा मोक्षदा नित्या तस्यै नित्यं नमोनमः॥

OBEISANCE TO YOU, THE MISTRESS OF THE GOD OF GODS; OBEISANCE TO YOU WHO ARE WORSHIPPED BY SHIVA; OBEISANCE ALWAYS, TO THE GODDESS WHO IS THE EMBODIMENT OF SPIRITUAL LOVE.

OBEISANCE ALWAYS TO THAT GODDESS WHO TAKES ONE TO THE OTHER SHORE OF BINDING SAMSARA, THE GREAT MOTHER, THE BESTOWER OF SPIRITUAL WISDOM AND DELIVERANCE, THE ETERNAL.

THE MATRIKABHELATANTRA
VII.15.17.

Acknowledgements

Years ago, Namita Gokhale had asked me to write about my life with Ma. That was the beginning. Since then, she has nourished this book, through all its stages, with her affection, wisdom and deep intuition.

My niece Janhavi Prasada, who has been a pillar of strength to me always, guided and inspired me at every step in the journey of this book. I owe so much to her.

Devapriya Roy brought her writerly perspective and understanding, and worked on this book with unparalleled dedication and love.

My publisher Meru Gokhale, with her fine eye for editing and brilliant insights, gave the book shape and direction.

Thank you, Rea Mukherjee and Binita Roy, for your help and support. Thank you, Ahlawat Gunjan and Akangksha Sarmah for the inspired cover design.

Acknowledgements

Thank you to all those who have given their insights, affection and support through the journey of the book.

Ma's blessings.

My gratitude.

Jaya Prasada
April 2022